By GILL

The Ultimate

A Fresh Guide to Delicious Dishes with Greens, Veggies, Grains, and Proteins

Connect with us!

@cook_your_book

● ●

TABLE OF CONTENTS

31 | Chapter 3, Vegan Salads

41 | Chapter 4, Grain Salads

52 | Chapter 5, Bean Salads

63 | Chapter 6, Fruit Salads

74 | Chapter 7, Special Occasion Salads

117 | Chapter 11, Healthy Salad Sauces

123 | Conclusion

125 | Appendix

Why do you need to eat salads?

Nutritional Benefits

Salads are rich in vitamins, minerals, and antioxidants that your body needs to function correctly. Leafy greens like spinach and kale provide essential nutrients such as vitamin K, vitamin A, and folate, while other ingredients like tomatoes, cucumbers, and peppers add vitamin C and hydration.

Low in Calories, High in Fiber

Salads are often low in calories but high in dietary fiber, which helps digestion, prevents constipation, and supports weight management. They make you feel full longer, reducing the urge to snack on unhealthy options.

Supports Overall Health

Regular consumption of salads can help reduce the risk of chronic diseases, such as heart disease, diabetes, and certain cancers. The variety of phytonutrients in fresh vegetables supports your immune system and reduces inflammation.

Customizable and Delicious

Salads can be tailored to your taste preferences and dietary needs, making them a versatile addition to your meals. Adding protein (like grilled chicken or beans) or healthy fats (like avocados or olive oil) turns a simple salad into a complete meal.

Healthy Ingredients

Leafy Greens & Colorful Vegetables
These should form the base of most salads. Options like spinach, arugula, kale, and romaine lettuce are packed with nutrients, including vitamins A, C, and K, folate, and iron. Include a variety of vegetables like carrots, bell peppers, cucumbers, and tomatoes. The more colors you add, the broader the range of nutrients and antioxidants you get.

Proteins
Add lean proteins like grilled chicken, turkey, boiled eggs, tofu, or legumes like chickpeas and lentils. These boost satiety and provide the amino acids needed for muscle repair and overall health.

Healthy Fats
Ingredients like avocados, nuts, seeds (such as sunflower or chia seeds), and olive oil offer essential fatty acids that support heart health and brain function.

Whole Grains and Beans
Quinoa, barley, or beans can make your salad heartier and more fiber-rich, promoting better digestion and providing long-lasting energy.

How to Choose Fresh Products

Look for Bright Colors

Fresh vegetables and fruits have vibrant, rich colors. Dull or faded produce may indicate it's past its prime. For example, greens should be crisp and deeply colored, and tomatoes should be firm and evenly red.

Check for Firmness and Texture

Pick produce that feels firm and heavy for its size. Avoid items with bruises, soft spots, or discoloration. For leafy greens, look for leaves without wilted edges or brown spots.

Smell the Produce

Fresh fruits and vegetables should have a natural, pleasant aroma. For instance, ripe melons should smell sweet at the stem end, while fresh herbs like basil should have a strong, fragrant scent.

Seasonality Matters

Buy seasonal produce whenever possible. Seasonal fruits and vegetables are usually fresher, tastier, and more nutritious. They're also more likely to be locally grown, reducing the environmental impact of transport.

Read Labels for Packaged Items

For pre-packaged salads or vegetables, check the expiration date and ensure there is no condensation or slimy texture inside the packaging.

Chapter 1

Salads with Meat

A Perfect Balance of Nutrition and Flavor

Salads with meat often incorporate complementary ingredients like creamy avocados, crunchy nuts, or tangy dressings to elevate the taste and texture. Some recipes include grains like quinoa or barley for added substance and fiber.

Perfect for health-conscious individuals, these salads are rich in nutrients, customizable to dietary preferences, and bursting with flavor. Whether served warm or cold, they offer a delightful mix of freshness and heartiness that satisfies both the palate and the appetite.

Caesar with chicken

Ingredients :

1 large head of romaine lettuce, washed and chopped

1/2 cup croutons (store-bought or homemade)

1/4 cup Parmesan cheese, shaved or grated

Procedure :

- Prepare the Dressing:

In a medium bowl, whisk together the mayonnaise, grated Parmesan cheese, lemon juice, Dijon mustard, Worcestershire sauce, minced garlic, salt, and black pepper.

If using anchovy fillets, mash them into a paste before adding them to the mixture. Stir well until creamy.

- Assemble the Salad:

Place the chopped romaine lettuce in a large bowl.

Drizzle the dressing over the lettuce and toss until evenly coated.

- Add Toppings:

Sprinkle the croutons and shaved Parmesan cheese on top.

- Serve immediately for the freshest flavor.

Nutritions

Calories per Serving: 210 kcal

Protein: 7 g

Fat: 16 g

Carbohydrates: 10 g

Prep Time	:	15 min
Cook Time	:	15 min
Servings	:	4 servings

Beef and Avocado Salad

Ingredients :

100g (3.5 oz) beef steak (e.g., sirloin or flank)

1/4 avocado, diced

1 cup mixed salad greens (spinach, arugula, or lettuce)

4 cherry tomatoes, halved

1 tablespoon red onion, thinly sliced

1 tablespoon crumbled feta cheese (optional)

1 teaspoon olive oil

1/2 teaspoon lemon juice

1/4 teaspoon Dijon mustard

1/4 teaspoon honey (optional)

A pinch of salt

A pinch of black pepper

Procedure :

- Cook the Beef:

Heat a small skillet or grill pan over medium-high heat.

Cook the beef for 2–3 minutes on each side for medium-rare, or adjust to your preferred doneness.

Let the steak rest for 3–5 minutes, then slice thinly against the grain.

- Prepare the Dressing:

In a small bowl, whisk together olive oil, lemon juice, Dijon mustard, honey (if using), salt, and black pepper.

- Assemble the Salad:

Place the mixed greens on a plate or in a bowl.

Add the diced avocado, cherry tomatoes, and red onion.

Drizzle the dressing over the salad.

- Serve.

Prep Time	:	10 min
Cook Time	:	5 min
Servings	:	1 serving

Nutritions

Calories per Serving: 320 kcal

Protein: 25 g

Fat: 22 g

Carbohydrates: 8 g

Chicken Salad with Walnuts

Ingredients :

100g (3.5 oz) cooked chicken breast, shredded or diced

1 cup mixed salad greens (spinach, arugula, or lettuce)

1/4 cup cucumber, diced

1/4 cup cherry tomatoes, halved

1 tablespoon red onion, thinly sliced

1 tablespoon walnuts, roughly chopped

1 tablespoon crumbled feta cheese (optional)

1 teaspoon olive oil

1 teaspoon lemon juice

1/2 teaspoon Dijon mustard

1/2 teaspoon honey (optional)

A pinch of salt

A pinch of black pepper

Nutritions

Calories per Serving: 280 kcal

Protein: 25 g

Fat: 16 g

Carbohydrates: 8 g

Procedure :

- Prepare the Chicken (if not pre-cooked):

Season a small chicken breast with salt and pepper.

Cook in a skillet over medium heat with 1 teaspoon olive oil for about 6–7 minutes per side, until fully cooked.

Let it cool, then shred or dice into bite-sized pieces.

- Make the Dressing:

In a small bowl, whisk together the olive oil and lemon juice until combined.

Add the Dijon mustard and honey (if using), and whisk until smooth and emulsified.

Season with a pinch of salt and black pepper to taste.

Taste and adjust seasoning if necessary.

- Add the Dressing.
- Serve.

Prep Time	:	10 min
Cook Time	:	10 min
Servings	:	1 serving

Turkey and Cranberry Salad

Ingredients :

100g (3.5 oz) cooked turkey breast, shredded or diced

1 cup mixed salad greens (spinach, arugula, or lettuce)

1/4 cup cucumber, diced

2 tablespoons dried cranberries

1 tablespoon walnuts or pecans, roughly chopped

1/4 cup cherry tomatoes, halved

1 tablespoon crumbled feta or goat cheese (optional)

1 teaspoon olive oil

1 teaspoon balsamic vinegar

1/2 teaspoon honey or maple syrup

1/4 teaspoon Dijon mustard

A pinch of salt

A pinch of black pepper

Nutritions

Calories per Serving: 320 kcal

Protein: 27 g

Fat: 14 g

Carbohydrates: 20 g

Procedure :

- Prepare the Turkey (if not pre-cooked):

Season a small turkey breast cutlet with salt and pepper.

Cook in a skillet over medium heat with 1 teaspoon olive oil for 6–8 minutes per side, until fully cooked.

Let it cool, then shred or dice into bite-sized pieces.

- Prepare the Dressing:

In a small bowl, whisk together olive oil, balsamic vinegar, honey, Dijon mustard, salt, and black pepper.

- Add the Dressing:

Drizzle the dressing over the salad. Toss gently to combine or serve as is.

- Assemble the Salad:

Put all the prepared ingredients in the bowl, whisk and enjoy.

- Serve.

Prep Time	:	10 min
Cook Time	:	10 min
Servings	:	1 serving

Meat salad with beans and corn

Ingredients :

100g (3.5 oz) cooked beef, chicken, or turkey, shredded or diced

1/4 cup canned black beans, rinsed and drained

1/4 cup canned corn, rinsed and drained

1 cup mixed salad greens (spinach, arugula, or lettuce)

1/4 cup cherry tomatoes, halved

1 tablespoon red onion, thinly sliced

1 tablespoon shredded cheddar or crumbled feta cheese (optional)

1 teaspoon olive oil

1 teaspoon lime juice

1/4 teaspoon ground cumin

1/4 teaspoon smoked paprika

A pinch of salt

A pinch of black pepper

Nutritions

Calories per Serving: 350 kcal

Protein: 28 g

Fat: 12 g

Carbohydrates: 30 g

Procedure :

- Prepare the Meat (if not pre-cooked): Season 100g of your chosen meat (beef, chicken, or turkey) with salt, pepper, and a pinch of cumin.

Cook in a skillet over medium heat with 1 teaspoon olive oil for about 6–8 minutes, or until fully cooked.

Let it cool slightly, then shred or dice into bite-sized pieces.

- Prepare the Dressing:

In a small bowl, whisk together olive oil, lime juice, ground cumin, smoked paprika, salt, and black pepper.

- Add the Dressing:

Drizzle the dressing over the salad. Toss gently to combine or serve layered for presentation.

- Assemble the Salad.
- Serve.

Prep Time	:	10 min
Cook Time	:	10 min
Servings	:	1 serving

Salad with chicken breasts and mango

Ingredients :

100g (3.5 oz) cooked chicken breast, sliced or diced

1/2 cup fresh mango, diced

1 cup mixed salad greens (spinach, arugula, or lettuce)

1/4 cup cucumber, diced

2 tablespoons red bell pepper, diced

1 tablespoon red onion, thinly sliced

1 tablespoon chopped cashews or almonds (optional)

1 teaspoon olive oil

1 teaspoon lime juice

1/2 teaspoon honey

A pinch of salt

A pinch of black pepper

Procedure :

- Prepare the Chicken (if not pre-cooked):

Season the chicken breast with salt and pepper.

Cook in a skillet over medium heat with 1 teaspoon olive oil for about 6–7 minutes per side, until fully cooked.

Let it cool slightly, then slice or dice into bite-sized pieces.

- Prepare the Dressing:

In a small bowl, whisk together olive oil, lime juice, honey, salt, and black pepper.

- Assemble the Salad.

- Add the Dressing:

Drizzle the dressing over the salad. Toss gently to combine or serve as is.

- Serve:

Enjoy immediately for a refreshing and nutritious meal.

Nutritions

Calories per Serving: 290 kcal

Protein: 25 g

Fat: 9 g

Carbohydrates: 25 g

Prep Time	:	10 min
Cook Time	:	10 min
Servings	:	1 serving

salad with duck and oranges

Ingredients :

100g (3.5 oz) cooked duck breast, thinly sliced

1/2 orange, peeled and segmented

1 cup mixed salad greens (arugula, spinach, or lettuce)

1/4 cup cucumber, thinly sliced

2 tablespoons red onion, thinly sliced

1 tablespoon slivered almonds or chopped walnuts (optional)

1 teaspoon olive oil

1 teaspoon orange juice (from the orange segments)

1/2 teaspoon balsamic vinegar

1/4 teaspoon Dijon mustard

A pinch of salt

A pinch of black pepper

Procedure :

- Prepare the Duck (if not pre-cooked):
Score the skin of the duck breast and season with salt and pepper.

Place the duck breast skin-side down in a cold skillet. Cook over medium heat for about 6–7 minutes, rendering the fat and crisping the skin.

Flip and cook for another 3–4 minutes for medium-rare or until desired doneness.

Let it rest for 5 minutes before slicing thinly.

- Prepare the Dressing:
In a small bowl, whisk together olive oil, orange juice, balsamic vinegar, Dijon mustard, salt, and black pepper.

- Assemble the Salad.
- Add the Dressing:
Drizzle the dressing over the salad.

Nutritions

Calories per Serving: 350 kcal

Protein: 25 g

Fat: 18 g

Carbohydrates: 15 g

Prep Time	:	10 min
Cook Time	:	10 min
Servings	:	1 serving

Salad with smoked pork and pineapple

Ingredients :

100g (3.5 oz) smoked pork, thinly sliced or diced

1/2 cup fresh pineapple, diced

1 cup mixed salad greens (spinach, arugula, or lettuce)

1/4 cup cherry tomatoes, halved

1/4 cup cucumber, diced

1 tablespoon red onion, thinly sliced

1 tablespoon chopped cashews or almonds (optional)

1 teaspoon olive oil

1 teaspoon pineapple juice (from the fresh pineapple)

1/2 teaspoon honey or maple syrup

1/4 teaspoon Dijon mustard

A pinch of salt

A pinch of black pepper

Nutritions

Calories per Serving: 320 kcal

Protein: 24 g

Fat: 14 g

Carbohydrates: 20 g

Procedure :

- Prepare the Pork:
Pat the pork dry with paper towels.
Rub it with olive oil to help the seasoning adhere.
- Season the Pork:
- In a small bowl, mix smoked paprika, garlic powder, onion powder, cumin, black pepper, salt, and cayenne (if using).
- Rub the spice mixture evenly over the pork, covering all sides.
- Preheat your smoker to 225°F (107°C).
- Add wood chips of your choice to infuse the pork with a smoky flavor.
- Place the pork on the smoker grates. Insert a meat thermometer into the thickest part of the meat.
- Smoke the pork until the internal temperature reaches 145°F (63°C) for tenderloin or 195°F (90°C) for shoulder (for shredding). This typically takes 1.5–3 hours.
- Remove the pork from the smoker and wrap it loosely in foil. Let it rest for 10–15 minutes to retain juices.
- Prepare the Dressing:
In a small bowl, whisk together olive oil, pineapple juice, honey, Dijon mustard, salt, and black pepper.
- Assemble the Salad:
Place the mixed salad greens on a plate or in a bowl.
Add the smoked pork, pineapple, cherry tomatoes, cucumber, and red onion.
Sprinkle with chopped nuts if desired for added crunch.
- Add the Dressing:
Drizzle the dressing over the salad. Toss gently to combine or serve layered for presentation.
- Serve:
Enjoy immediately for a tropical-inspired meal with a smoky twist.

Prep Time	:	10 min
Cook Time	:	10 min
Servings	:	1 serving

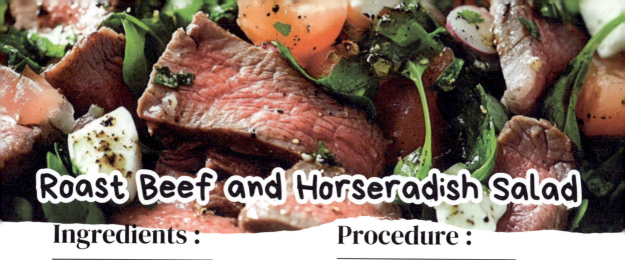

Roast Beef and Horseradish salad

Ingredients :

100g (3.5 oz) thinly sliced roast beef

(store-bought or homemade)

2 cups mixed salad greens (arugula,

spinach, or lettuce)

1/4 cup cherry tomatoes, halved

1/4 cup cucumber, sliced

1 tablespoon red onion, thinly sliced

1 tablespoon capers or pickled onions

(optional)

1 teaspoon prepared horseradish

1 teaspoon Greek yogurt or sour cream

1 teaspoon olive oil

1 teaspoon lemon juice

A pinch of salt

A pinch of black pepper

Nutritions

Calories per Serving: 250 kcal

Protein: 26 g

Fat: 12 g

Carbohydrates: 8 g

Procedure :

- Prepare the Beef:
Preheat your oven to 450°F (232°C).
Pat the beef dry with paper towels. Rub it all over with olive oil.
In a small bowl, mix salt, pepper, garlic powder, thyme, paprika, and onion powder.
Rub the seasoning mixture evenly over the beef, covering all sides.
Heat a large oven-safe skillet or roasting pan over medium-high heat.
Sear the beef for 2–3 minutes per side until browned to lock in the flavor.
Transfer the skillet or roasting pan to the preheated oven. Roast the beef for:
20–25 minutes for medium-rare (internal temperature of 130–135°F / 54–57°C).
25–30 minutes for medium (135–140°F / 57–60°C).
- Prepare the Dressing:
In a small bowl, whisk together horseradish, Greek yogurt (or sour cream), olive oil, lemon juice, salt, and black pepper until smooth.
- Assemble the Salad:
Arrange the mixed salad greens on a plate or in a bowl.
Add the roast beef slices, cherry tomatoes, cucumber, and red onion.
Sprinkle with capers or pickled onions, if using.
- Add the Dressing:
Drizzle the horseradish dressing over the salad. Toss gently to combine or serve layered for presentation.
- Serve:
Enjoy immediately for a refreshing and flavorful meal.

Prep Time	:	10 min
Cook Time	:	10 min
Servings	:	1 serving

Chapter 2

Seafood Salads

A Taste of the Ocean in Every Bite

From a classic shrimp cocktail salad to a Mediterranean-inspired octopus creation or a creamy crab and avocado blend, these recipes highlight seafood's natural sweetness and brininess. Balanced with citrusy vinaigrettes, creamy sauces, or spicy accents, each salad is a delightful harmony of flavors and textures.

Seafood salads are easy to prepare and endlessly customizable, perfect for summer picnics, elegant dinner parties, or a casual weekday treat. Dive into this section to explore the art of creating delicious, ocean-inspired dishes that will leave you and your guests craving more.

Tuna and Egg Salad

Ingredients :

1 boiled egg, peeled and chopped

1/2 cup canned tuna in water, drained

1 cup mixed salad greens (spinach, arugula, or lettuce)

1/4 cup cucumber, diced

1/4 cup cherry tomatoes, halved

1 tablespoon red onion, finely chopped

1 teaspoon capers (optional)

1 teaspoon olive oil

1 teaspoon lemon juice

1/2 teaspoon Dijon mustard

A pinch of salt

A pinch of black pepper

Procedure :

- Prepare the Egg:

Place the egg in a saucepan and cover with water.

Bring to a boil, then lower the heat and simmer for 8–10 minutes for a hard-boiled egg.

Cool under cold running water, peel, and chop.

- Prepare the Dressing:

In a small bowl, whisk together olive oil, lemon juice, Dijon mustard, salt, and black pepper.

- Assemble the Salad:

Place the mixed salad greens in a bowl or on a plate.

Add the drained tuna, chopped boiled egg, cucumber, cherry tomatoes, and red onion.

- Add the Dressing.
- Serve.

Nutritions

Calories per Serving: 280 kcal

Protein: 30 g

Fat: 14 g

Carbohydrates: 6 g

Prep Time	:	10 min
Cook Time	:	10 min
Servings	:	1 serving

Greek salad with shrimps

Ingredients :

100g (3.5 oz) cooked shrimp, peeled and deveined

1 cup romaine lettuce or mixed greens

1/4 cup cherry tomatoes, halved

1/4 cup cucumber, diced

2 tablespoons red onion, thinly sliced

2 tablespoons Kalamata olives, pitted and halved

2 tablespoons crumbled feta cheese

1 teaspoon olive oil

1 teaspoon red wine vinegar

1/4 teaspoon dried oregano

A pinch of salt

A pinch of black pepper

Procedure :

- Cook the Shrimp (if not pre-cooked):

Heat a skillet over medium heat with a drizzle of olive oil.

Season the shrimp lightly with salt and pepper.

Cook for 2–3 minutes per side until pink and fully cooked. Let cool slightly.

- Prepare the Dressing:

In a small bowl, whisk together olive oil, red wine vinegar, dried oregano, salt, and black pepper.

- Assemble the Salad:

Place the romaine lettuce or mixed greens on a plate or in a bowl.

Add the cherry tomatoes, cucumber, red onion, Kalamata olives, and feta cheese. Top with the cooked shrimp.

- Add the Dressing.
- Serve.

Nutritions

Calories per Serving: 280 kcal

Protein: 24 g

Fat: 15 g

Carbohydrates: 10 g

Prep Time	:	10 min
Cook Time	:	5 min
Servings	:	1 serving

Salmon and Avocado Salad

Ingredients :

100g (3.5 oz) cooked salmon (grilled, baked, or smoked), flaked

1/2 avocado, sliced

1 cup mixed salad greens (arugula, spinach, or lettuce)

1/4 cup cucumber, diced

1/4 cup cherry tomatoes, halved

1 tablespoon red onion, thinly sliced

1 teaspoon sesame seeds or chopped nuts (optional)

1 teaspoon olive oil

1 teaspoon lemon juice

1/2 teaspoon Dijon mustard

A pinch of salt

A pinch of black pepper

Procedure :

- Prepare the Salmon (if not pre-cooked):

Season a 100g piece of salmon with salt, pepper, and a drizzle of olive oil.

Bake at 400°F (200°C) for 10–12 minutes or grill for 3–4 minutes per side until fully cooked.

Let cool slightly, then flake with a fork.

- Prepare the Dressing:

In a small bowl, whisk together olive oil, lemon juice, Dijon mustard, salt, and black pepper.

- Assemble the Salad.
- Add the Dressing.

Drizzle the dressing over the salad. Toss gently to combine or serve layered for presentation.

- Serve.

Nutritions

Calories per Serving: 350 kcal

Protein: 26 g

Fat: 22 g

Carbohydrates: 10 g

Prep Time	:	10 min
Cook Time	:	10 min
Servings	:	1 serving

Salad with squid and lemon

Ingredients :

100g (3.5 oz) squid, cleaned and sliced into rings or tubes

2 cups mixed salad greens (arugula, spinach, or lettuce)

1/4 cup cucumber, sliced

1/4 cup cherry tomatoes, halved

1 tablespoon red onion, thinly sliced

1 tablespoon fresh parsley, chopped

1 tablespoon olives (optional)

1 teaspoon olive oil

1 teaspoon lemon juice (freshly squeezed)

Zest of 1/2 lemon

A pinch of salt

A pinch of black pepper

Procedure :

- Cook the Squid:

Heat a non-stick skillet over medium-high heat. Add a drizzle of olive oil.

Add the squid rings and cook for about 2-3 minutes, stirring frequently, until the squid is opaque and tender (be careful not to overcook).

Remove from heat and set aside to cool slightly.

- Prepare the Dressing:

In a small bowl, whisk together olive oil, lemon juice, lemon zest, salt, and black pepper until well combined.

- Assemble the Salad.

- Add the Dressing:

Drizzle the dressing over the salad. Toss gently to combine or serve layered for presentation.

- Serve.

Nutritions

Calories per Serving: 220 kcal

Protein: 23 g

Fat: 12 g

Carbohydrates: 8 g

Prep Time	:	10 min
Cook Time	:	5 min
Servings	:	1 serving

Salad with herring and potatoes

Ingredients :

100g (3.5 oz) pickled or smoked herring, cut into bite-sized pieces

1 medium potato, boiled and diced

1/2 cup mixed salad greens (arugula, spinach, or lettuce)

1/4 cup cucumber, diced

1/4 cup cherry tomatoes, halved

1 tablespoon red onion, thinly sliced

1 boiled egg, peeled and sliced (optional)

Fresh dill, chopped (for garnish)

1 teaspoon olive oil

1 teaspoon apple cider vinegar or white wine vinegar

1 teaspoon Dijon mustard

A pinch of salt

A pinch of black pepper

Nutritions

Calories per Serving: 320 kcal

Protein: 18 g

Fat: 15 g

Carbohydrates: 28 g

Procedure :

- Prepare the Potatoes and Egg:

Peel and dice the potato, then place it in a saucepan. Cover with water and bring to a boil. Simmer for about 10 minutes until tender. Drain and let cool slightly.

If using a boiled egg, place it in a pot of boiling water for 8-10 minutes, then cool under cold running water, peel, and slice.

- Prepare the Dressing:

In a small bowl, whisk together olive oil, vinegar, Dijon mustard, salt, and black pepper until well combined.

- Assemble the Salad.

- Add the Dressing:

Drizzle the dressing over the salad. Toss gently to combine.

Garnish with chopped fresh dill for an added burst of flavor.

- Serve.

Prep Time	:	**10 min**
Cook Time	:	**15 min**
Servings	:	**1 serving**

Salad with mussels and greens

Ingredients :

100g (3.5 oz) cooked mussels (fresh or frozen, thawed if necessary)

2 cups mixed salad greens (arugula, spinach, or lettuce)

1/4 cup cucumber, sliced

1/4 cup cherry tomatoes, halved

1 tablespoon red onion, thinly sliced

1 tablespoon fresh parsley or cilantro, chopped

1 tablespoon olives (optional)

1 teaspoon olive oil

1 teaspoon lemon juice (freshly squeezed)

1/4 teaspoon Dijon mustard

A pinch of salt

A pinch of black pepper

Procedure :

• Prepare the Mussels (if necessary):
If your mussels are cooked and ready to eat, simply thaw them if frozen.
If you need to cook them, steam or heat the mussels in a covered pot for about 5 minutes until they open. Remove from heat, discard any mussels that didn't open, and set the cooked mussels aside to cool slightly.

• Prepare the Dressing:
In a small bowl, whisk together olive oil, lemon juice, Dijon mustard, salt, and black pepper until well combined.

• Assemble the Salad.

• Add the Dressing:
Drizzle the dressing over the salad. Toss gently to combine.

• Serve.

Nutritions

Calories per Serving: 250 kcal

Protein: 22 g

Fat: 12 g

Carbohydrates: 8 g

Prep Time	:	10 min
Cook Time	:	5 min
Servings	:	1 serving

Smoked Salmon and Cucumber Salad

Ingredients :

100g (3.5 oz) smoked salmon, sliced

1/2 cucumber, thinly sliced

1 cup mixed salad greens (arugula, spinach, or lettuce)

1/4 red onion, thinly sliced

1 tablespoon capers (optional)

1 tablespoon fresh dill, chopped

1 teaspoon olive oil

1 teaspoon lemon juice (freshly squeezed)

1/2 teaspoon Dijon mustard

A pinch of salt

A pinch of black pepper

Smoked paprika

Garlic powder

Onion powder

Brown sugar

Nutritions

Calories per Serving: 280 kcal

Protein: 20 g

Fat: 18 g

Carbohydrates: 8 g

Procedure :

- Prepare the Salmon:
Pat the salmon fillet dry with paper towels and brush it with olive oil.
Mix smoked paprika, garlic powder, onion powder, salt, pepper, and brown sugar (if using) in a small bowl. Rub this mixture evenly over the salmon.
Preheat your smoker to 225°F (107°C).
Add wood chips of your choice to create a gentle, aromatic smoke.
Place the salmon fillet directly on the smoker rack or on a piece of foil for easy handling.
Smoke the salmon until it reaches an internal temperature of 145°F (63°C) and flakes easily with a fork. This usually takes 1–2 hours, depending on the thickness of the fillet.
- Rest and Cool.
- Prepare the Dressing:
In a small bowl, whisk together olive oil, lemon juice, Dijon mustard, salt, and black pepper until well combined.
- Assemble the Salad:
Place the mixed salad greens on a plate or in a bowl.
Add the cucumber slices, red onion, and capers (if using).
Layer the smoked salmon on top of the salad and sprinkle with fresh dill.
- Add the Dressing:
Drizzle the dressing over the salad and toss gently to combine, or serve layered for presentation.
- Serve:
Enjoy immediately for a fresh, flavorful meal!

Prep Time	:	10 min
Cook Time	:	10 min
Servings	:	1 serving

Salad with anchovies and tomatoes

Ingredients :

4-6 anchovy fillets (packed in oil or salt, depending on preference)

1 medium tomato, diced or sliced

1/2 cup mixed salad greens (arugula, spinach, or lettuce)

1/4 red onion, thinly sliced

1 tablespoon capers (optional)

1 tablespoon black olives, sliced (optional)

Fresh parsley or basil, chopped (for garnish)

1 teaspoon olive oil

1 teaspoon red wine vinegar

1/4 teaspoon Dijon mustard

A pinch of salt

A pinch of black pepper

Nutritions

Calories per Serving: 220 kcal

Protein: 10 g

Fat: 15 g

Carbohydrates: 7 g

Procedure :

- Prepare the Anchovies:

If using salt-packed anchovies, rinse them thoroughly under cold water to remove excess salt. Pat them dry with a paper towel.

If using oil-packed anchovies, simply drain the fillets and pat them dry.

- Prepare the Dressing:

In a small bowl, whisk together olive oil, red wine vinegar, Dijon mustard, salt, and black pepper until well combined.

- Assemble the Salad:

Place the mixed salad greens on a plate or in a bowl.

Add the diced or sliced tomato, red onion, capers (if using), and black olives (optional).

Arrange the anchovy fillets on top of the salad.

- Add the Dressing:

Drizzle the dressing over the salad. Toss gently to combine or serve layered for presentation.

- Serve.

Prep Time	:	10 min
Cook Time	:	10 min
Servings	:	1 serving

Salad with fish and mango

Ingredients :

100g (3.5 oz) white fish fillet (such as tilapia, cod, or snapper), grilled or pan-seared

1/2 ripe mango, peeled and diced

1 cup mixed salad greens (arugula, spinach, or lettuce)

1/4 cucumber, sliced

1/4 red bell pepper, thinly sliced

1 tablespoon red onion, thinly sliced

1 tablespoon fresh cilantro or mint, chopped

1 teaspoon olive oil

1 teaspoon lime juice (freshly squeezed)

1/2 teaspoon honey or agave syrup

A pinch of salt

A pinch of black pepper

Nutritions

Calories per Serving: 290 kcal

Protein: 25 g

Fat: 12 g

Carbohydrates: 20 g

Procedure :

- Prepare the Fish:

Season the fish fillet with salt and pepper.
Heat a non-stick skillet over medium heat and add a small amount of olive oil.
Cook the fish for about 2-3 minutes per side until fully cooked and flakey.
Alternatively, you can grill or bake the fish.
Once cooked, break the fish into bite-sized pieces and set aside to cool slightly.

- Prepare the Dressing:

In a small bowl, whisk together olive oil, lime juice, honey, salt, and black pepper until the dressing is well combined.

- Assemble the Salad.
- Add the Dressing:
- Drizzle the dressing over the salad and toss gently to combine.
- Serve.

Prep Time	:	10 min
Cook Time	:	5-7 min
Servings	:	1 serving

Seafood Salad with Chili Sauce

Ingredients :

100g (3.5 oz) mixed seafood (such as shrimp, squid, and scallops), cooked

1 cup mixed salad greens (arugula, spinach, or lettuce)

1/4 cucumber, sliced

1/4 red bell pepper, thinly sliced

1/4 small red onion, thinly sliced

1 tablespoon fresh cilantro or parsley, chopped

1 tablespoon avocado, diced (optional)

1 tablespoon chili sauce (preferably Thai or Sriracha)

1 teaspoon soy sauce

1 teaspoon lime juice

1 teaspoon honey or agave syrup

1 teaspoon sesame oil (optional)

Procedure :

• Prepare the Seafood:

If your seafood is not pre-cooked, boil or steam the shrimp, squid, and scallops for about 2-3 minutes until opaque and cooked through. Drain and set aside to cool slightly.

If using frozen seafood, thaw and cook according to package instructions.

• Prepare the Chili Sauce Dressing:

In a small bowl, whisk together chili sauce, soy sauce, lime juice, honey, and sesame oil (if using) until the dressing is well combined.

• Assemble the Salad.

• Add the Dressing:

Drizzle the chili sauce dressing over the salad and toss gently to combine.

• Serve.

Nutritions

Calories per Serving: 280 kcal

Protein: 25 g

Fat: 15 g

Carbohydrates: 12 g

Prep Time :	10 min
Cook Time :	5 min
Servings :	1 serving

Chapter 3

Vegan Salads

Fresh, Flavorful, and Nourishing

From crisp green salads to creative grain bowls and vibrant quinoa blends to hearty bean salads, this collection showcases the versatility and beauty of plant-based ingredients. Each recipe is designed to be a feast for the senses, with bold dressings, zesty vinaigrettes, and creamy avocado or hummus toppings, adding a layer of richness and depth. Perfect for light lunches, meal prepping, or as a side dish to complement any main course, these vegan salads are designed to be easy to make, incredibly flavorful, and full of wholesome ingredients that support your health and well-being.

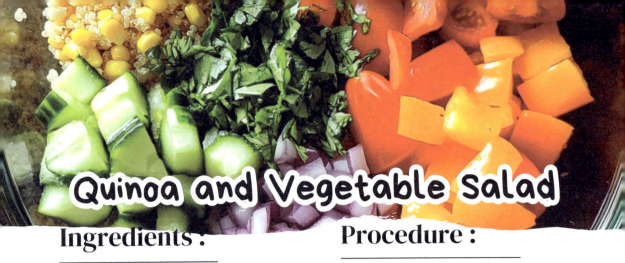

Quinoa and Vegetable Salad

Ingredients :

1/4 cup quinoa (uncooked)

1/2 cup cherry tomatoes, halved

1/4 cucumber, diced

1/4 red bell pepper, diced

1/4 cup corn kernels (fresh or frozen)

1/4 small red onion, finely chopped

1 tablespoon fresh parsley or cilantro, chopped

1 tablespoon olive oil

1 tablespoon lemon juice (freshly squeezed)

1/2 teaspoon Dijon mustard

A pinch of salt

A pinch of black pepper

Procedure :

- Cook the Quinoa:

Rinse the quinoa under cold water to remove any bitter coating.

In a small saucepan, combine 1/2 cup water with the quinoa. Bring it to a boil, then reduce the heat to low. Cover and simmer for about 12-15 minutes, or until the quinoa is tender and the water has been absorbed.

Remove from heat and let it sit, covered, for about 5 minutes. Fluff with a fork and let it cool slightly.

- Prepare the Dressing:

In a small bowl, whisk together olive oil, lemon juice, Dijon mustard, salt, and black pepper until well combined.

- Assemble the Salad.

- Add the Dressing.

- Serve.

Nutritions

Calories per Serving: 300 kcal

Protein: 8 g

Fat: 14 g

Carbohydrates: 36 g

Prep Time	:	**10 min**
Cook Time	:	**15 min**
Servings	:	**1 serving**

Greek Salad with Tofu

Ingredients :

1 cup cherry tomatoes, halved

1/2 cucumber, diced

1/4 red onion, thinly sliced

1/4 green bell pepper, thinly sliced

5-6 kalamata olives

1 oz (30g) tofu , crumbled or cubed

1 tablespoon fresh parsley or oregano, chopped

1 tablespoon olive oil

1 teaspoon red wine vinegar

1/4 teaspoon dried oregano

A pinch of salt

A pinch of black pepper

Procedure :

- Prepare the Dressing:

In a small bowl, whisk together olive oil, red wine vinegar, dried oregano, salt, and black pepper until the dressing is well combined.

- Assemble the Salad:

In a medium-sized bowl or plate, combine the cherry tomatoes, cucumber, red onion, green bell pepper, and kalamata olives. Add the crumbled or cubed tofu on top.

- Add the Dressing:

Drizzle the dressing over the salad and toss gently to combine, or leave it layered for presentation.

- Garnish and Serve:

Sprinkle with fresh parsley or oregano. Serve immediately as a refreshing and savory meal or side dish.

Nutritions

Calories per Serving: 250 kcal

Protein: 6 g

Fat: 20 g

Carbohydrates: 8 g

Prep Time	:	**10 min**
Cook Time	:	**10 min**
Servings	:	**1 serving**

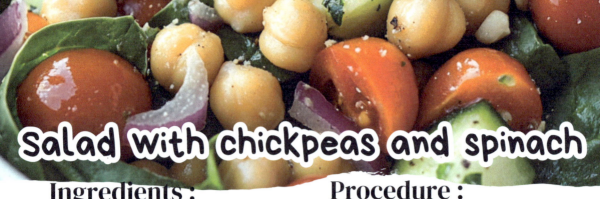

Salad with chickpeas and spinach

Ingredients :

1 cup fresh spinach leaves, washed and dried

1/2 cup canned chickpeas, rinsed and drained

1/4 cucumber, diced

1/4 cup cherry tomatoes, halved

1 tablespoon red onion, finely chopped

1 tablespoon sunflower seeds or chopped walnuts (optional)

1 tablespoon olive oil

1 teaspoon lemon juice

1/4 teaspoon Dijon mustard

1/4 teaspoon ground cumin (optional, for extra flavor)

A pinch of salt

A pinch of black pepper

Procedure :

- Prepare the Dressing:

In a small bowl, whisk together olive oil, lemon juice, Dijon mustard, ground cumin (if using), salt, and black pepper until the dressing is well combined.

- Assemble the Salad:

In a bowl or on a plate, arrange the spinach leaves.

Add the chickpeas, diced cucumber, cherry tomatoes, and red onion.

Sprinkle with sunflower seeds or chopped walnuts for added crunch and flavor (optional).

- Add the Dressing:

Drizzle the dressing over the salad and toss gently to combine.

- Serve:

Enjoy immediately as a nutritious and protein-packed meal or side dish.

Nutritions

Calories per Serving: 280 kcal

Protein: 9 g

Fat: 14 g

Carbohydrates: 28 g

Prep Time	:	10 min
Cook Time	:	10 min
Servings	:	1 serving

Salad with avocado and tomatoes

Ingredients :

1/2 ripe avocado, diced

1 cup cherry tomatoes, halved (or 1 medium tomato, diced)

1/4 red onion, thinly sliced

1 tablespoon fresh cilantro or parsley, chopped

1 cup mixed greens (optional, for added volume)

1 tablespoon olive oil

1 teaspoon lime juice (freshly squeezed)

1/2 teaspoon honey (optional, for slight sweetness)

A pinch of salt

A pinch of black pepper

Procedure :

- Prepare the Dressing:

In a small bowl, whisk together olive oil, lime juice, honey (if using), salt, and black pepper until the dressing is well combined.

- Assemble the Salad:

In a bowl or on a plate, combine the diced avocado, halved cherry tomatoes, and red onion.

If using mixed greens, arrange them as a base before adding the avocado and tomato mixture.

Sprinkle with fresh cilantro or parsley for garnish.

- Add the Dressing:

Drizzle the dressing over the salad and toss gently to combine.

- Serve.

Nutritions

Calories per Serving: 230 kcal

Protein: 3 g

Fat: 20 g

Carbohydrates: 10 g

Prep Time	:	10 min
Cook Time	:	10 min
Servings	:	1 serving

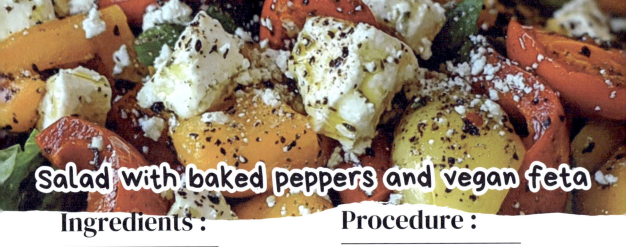

Salad with baked peppers and vegan feta

Ingredients :

1 medium red or yellow bell pepper

1/2 cup mixed greens (arugula, spinach, or lettuce)

1 oz (30g) vegan feta cheese, crumbled or cubed

1 tablespoon fresh parsley or basil, chopped

1 tablespoon olive oil

1 teaspoon balsamic vinegar

1/4 teaspoon Dijon mustard (optional)

A pinch of salt

A pinch of black pepper

Procedure :

- Bake the Pepper:

Preheat your oven to 400°F (200°C). Place the bell pepper on a baking sheet and roast for 12-15 minutes, turning halfway through, until the skin is slightly charred and the pepper is tender. Remove the pepper from the oven and let it cool slightly. Peel off the skin, remove the seeds, and slice into strips.

- Prepare the Dressing:

In a small bowl, whisk together olive oil, balsamic vinegar, Dijon mustard (if using), salt, and black pepper until smooth.

- Assemble the Salad.
- Add the Dressing.
- Serve:

Enjoy immediately for a flavorful and nutritious dish!

Nutritions

Calories per Serving: 200 kcal

Protein: 5 g

Fat: 15 g

Carbohydrates: 10 g

Prep Time	:	5 min
Cook Time	:	15 min
Servings	:	1 serving

Salad with broccoli and almonds

Ingredients :

1 cup broccoli florets

1/4 cup red bell pepper, diced (optional for color and sweetness)

1 tablespoon sliced almonds, toasted

1 tablespoon dried cranberries or raisins (optional)

1 tablespoon olive oil

1 teaspoon lemon juice

1/2 teaspoon honey (or maple syrup)

A pinch of salt

A pinch of black pepper

Procedure :

- Prepare the Broccoli:

Bring a small pot of water to a boil and add a pinch of salt.

Add the broccoli florets and blanch them for 2 minutes until they turn bright green and are slightly tender.

Drain the broccoli and rinse under cold water to stop the cooking process. Set aside to cool.

- Toast the Almonds.
- Prepare the Dressing:

In a small bowl, whisk together olive oil, lemon juice, honey, salt, and black pepper until well combined.

- Assemble the Salad.
- Drizzle the dressing.
- Serve.

Nutritions

Calories per Serving: 190 kcal

Protein: 5 g

Fat: 12 g

Carbohydrates: 15 g

Prep Time	:	10 min
Cook Time	:	5 min
Servings	:	1 serving

Beetroot and Tofu Salad

Ingredients :

1 small cooked beetroot, peeled and sliced into wedges

1 cup mixed greens (arugula, spinach, or lettuce)

1 oz (30g) tofu, crumbled

1 tablespoon walnuts, toasted and chopped (optional)

1 tablespoon olive oil

1 teaspoon balsamic vinegar

1/2 teaspoon honey (optional)

A pinch of salt

A pinch of black pepper

Procedure :

• Prepare the Dressing:

In a small bowl, whisk together olive oil, balsamic vinegar, honey (if using), salt, and black pepper until smooth.

• Assemble the Salad:

Arrange the mixed greens on a plate or in a bowl.

Top with beetroot wedges and crumbled tofu.

Sprinkle with toasted walnuts if desired for added crunch and flavor.

• Add the Dressing:

Drizzle the dressing over the salad and toss gently to coat.

• Serve:

Enjoy immediately for a flavorful and elegant dish!

Nutritions

Calories per Serving: 220 kcal

Protein: 6 g

Fat: 15 g

Carbohydrates: 14 g

Prep Time : 10 min

Cook Time : 10 min

Servings : 1 serving

Thai-Inspired Peanut Salad

Ingredients :

Mixed greens (e.g., romaine, spinach, or arugula): 2 cups

Shredded carrots: 1/4 cup

Red bell pepper (thinly sliced): 1/4 cup

Cucumber (sliced into thin rounds): 1/4 cup

Fresh cilantro (chopped): 1 tablespoon

Crushed peanuts: 1 tablespoon

Peanut butter (smooth): 1 tablespoon

Soy sauce: 1 teaspoon

Lime juice: 1 teaspoon (freshly squeezed)

Honey or maple syrup: 1/2 teaspoon

Sesame oil: 1/2 teaspoon

Water: 1-2 teaspoons (to thin the dressing)

Optional: A pinch of red pepper flakes for spice

Procedure :

- Prepare the Salad:

In a large bowl, combine the mixed greens, shredded carrots, red bell pepper, cucumber, and cilantro. Toss gently to mix.

- Make the Peanut Dressing:

In a small bowl, whisk together the peanut butter, soy sauce, lime juice, honey or maple syrup, sesame oil, and water. Adjust the consistency by adding more water if needed. If you like spice, add a pinch of red pepper flakes.

- Assemble the Salad:

Drizzle the peanut dressing over the salad and toss gently to coat the vegetables evenly.

- Garnish.

- Serve.

Nutritions

Calories per Serving: 210 kcal

Protein: 6 g

Fat: 14 g

Carbohydrates: 16 g

Prep Time	:	10 min
Cook Time	:	10 min
Servings	:	1 serving

Cauliflower and Raisin Salad

Ingredients :

1 cup cauliflower florets (raw or lightly steamed)

1 tablespoon raisins

1 tablespoon sliced almonds or sunflower seeds (optional)

1/4 cup red onion, thinly sliced (optional for extra flavor)

1 tablespoon olive oil

1 teaspoon lemon juice

1/2 teaspoon honey or maple syrup

A pinch of salt

A pinch of black pepper

Procedure :

- Prepare the Cauliflower:

Use raw cauliflower florets for a crunchy texture, or lightly steam them for 1–2 minutes to soften. Let cool if steamed.

- Prepare the Dressing:

In a small bowl, whisk together olive oil, lemon juice, honey, salt, and black pepper until smooth.

- Assemble the Salad:

In a bowl, combine the cauliflower florets, raisins, and sliced almonds or sunflower seeds (if using). Add the red onion slices if desired.

- Add the Dressing:

Drizzle the dressing over the salad and toss gently to coat.

- Serve:

Enjoy immediately for a fresh and flavorful dish!

Nutritions

Calories per Serving: 170 kcal

Protein: 3 g

Fat: 10 g

Carbohydrates: 18 g

Prep Time	:	**10 min**
Cook Time	:	**1-2 min**
Servings	:	**1 serving**

Chapter 4

Grain Salads

Hearty, Wholesome, and Flavorful

Grain salads combine the satisfying texture of grains like quinoa, farro, bulgur, and rice with vibrant vegetables, fresh herbs, and bold dressings. Perfect as a side dish or a standalone meal, these salads are endlessly versatile and packed with nutrients. Whether you're craving something light and zesty or hearty and comforting, grain salads deliver a delicious balance of flavor, texture, and nourishment.

Salad with bulgur and vegetables

Ingredients :

Bulgur: 1/4 cup (dry)

Cherry tomatoes: 5-6, halved

Cucumber: 1/4, diced

Bell pepper (any color): 1/4, diced

Red onion: 1 tablespoon, finely chopped

Fresh parsley: 2 tablespoons, chopped

Fresh mint (optional): 1 tablespoon, chopped

Olive oil: 1 teaspoon

Lemon juice: 1 tablespoon

Salt: to taste

Black pepper: to taste

Procedure :

- Cook the Bulgur:

Rinse the bulgur under cold water.

In a small saucepan, bring 1/2 cup of water to a boil.

Add the bulgur, reduce the heat to low, and cover.

Cook for about 10-12 minutes or until the water is absorbed and the bulgur is tender.

Fluff with a fork and let it cool.

- Prepare the Vegetables.
- Combine the Ingredients:
- In a bowl, mix the cooled bulgur with the chopped vegetables and herbs.
- Dress the Salad:

Drizzle olive oil and lemon juice over the salad.

Season with salt and black pepper to taste.

- Toss gently to combine.
- Serve.

Nutritions

Calories per Serving: 180 kcal

Protein: 5 g

Fat: 5 g

Carbohydrates: 30 g

Prep Time	:	10 min
Cook Time	:	12 min
Servings	:	1 serving

Salad with rice and chicken

Ingredients :

Cooked rice: 1/2 cup (preferably cooled, any variety)

Cooked chicken breast: 3 oz (shredded or diced)

Cherry tomatoes: 5-6, halved

Cucumber: 1/4, diced

Bell pepper (any color): 1/4, diced

Red onion: 1 tablespoon, finely chopped

Fresh parsley: 1 tablespoon, chopped

Olive oil: 1 teaspoon

Lemon juice: 1 tablespoon

Salt: to taste

Black pepper: to taste

Paprika or chili flakes (optional): 1/4 teaspoon

Procedure :

- Prepare the Chicken:

If you don't have pre-cooked chicken, season a small chicken breast with salt and pepper, cook it in a skillet with a teaspoon of olive oil for about 5-7 minutes per side until fully cooked. Let it cool slightly, then shred or dice it.

- Prepare the Rice:

If not already cooked, rinse 1/4 cup of dry rice.

Cook it in 1/2 cup of water until tender (about 15 minutes).

Let it cool.

- Chop the Vegetables:

Dice the cucumber, bell pepper, and red onion. Halve the cherry tomatoes. Chop the parsley.

- Combine the Ingredients.
- Dress the Salad.
- Serve.

Nutritions

Calories per Serving: 320 kcal

Protein: 25 g

Fat: 7 g

Carbohydrates: 35 g

Prep Time	:	10 min
Cook Time	:	15 min
Servings	:	1 serving

Salad with pearl barley and greens

Ingredients :

Pearl barley: 1/4 cup (dry)

Mixed greens (e.g., spinach, arugula, kale): 1 cup

Cherry tomatoes: 5-6, halved

Cucumber: 1/4, diced

Feta cheese: 1 tablespoon, crumbled (optional)

Fresh parsley: 1 tablespoon, chopped

Olive oil: 1 teaspoon

Lemon juice: 1 tablespoon

Salt: to taste

Black pepper: to taste

Procedure :

• Cook the Pearl Barley:

Rinse the pearl barley under cold water.

In a small saucepan, bring 3/4 cup of water to a boil.

Add the pearl barley, reduce the heat to low, and simmer for 25-30 minutes, or until tender. Drain and let it cool.

• Prepare the Greens and Vegetables:

Wash and dry the greens. Chop the cucumber and halve the cherry tomatoes.

• Combine the Salad:

In a large bowl, mix the cooled pearl barley, mixed greens, cherry tomatoes, cucumber, and parsley. Add feta cheese if desired.

• Dress the Salad.

• Serve:

Transfer the salad to a serving plate and enjoy fresh.

Nutritions

Calories per Serving: 230 kcal

Protein: 6 g

Fat: 5 g

Carbohydrates: 40 g

Prep Time	:	10 min
Cook Time	:	30 min
Servings	:	1 serving

salad with buckwheat and mushrooms

Ingredients :

Buckwheat: 1/4 cup (dry)

Mushrooms (button, cremini, or your choice): 1/2 cup, sliced

Garlic: 1 small clove, minced

Olive oil: 1 teaspoon

Mixed greens (e.g., spinach or arugula): 1 cup

Red onion: 1 tablespoon, finely chopped

Fresh parsley: 1 tablespoon, chopped

Lemon juice: 1 tablespoon

Salt: to taste

Black pepper: to taste

Optional toppings: 1 teaspoon sunflower seeds or crushed walnuts

Nutritions

Calories per Serving: 250 kcal

Protein: 7 g

Fat: 6 g

Carbohydrates: 40 g

Procedure :

• Cook the Buckwheat:

Rinse the buckwheat under cold water.

In a small saucepan, bring 1/2 cup of water to a boil.

Add the buckwheat, reduce heat to low, and simmer for 15 minutes, or until tender and the water is absorbed. Fluff with a fork and let it cool.

• Sauté the Mushrooms:

Heat the olive oil in a skillet over medium heat.

Add the mushrooms and garlic, cooking until the mushrooms are tender and lightly browned (about 5 minutes). Season with a pinch of salt and pepper. Let them cool slightly.

• Prepare the Vegetables.

• Dress the Salad.

• Serve.

Prep Time	:	10 min
Cook Time	:	20 min
Servings	:	1 serving

Quinoa and Avocado Salad

Ingredients :

Quinoa: 1/4 cup (dry)

Avocado: 1/2, diced

Cherry tomatoes: 5-6, halved

Cucumber: 1/4, diced

Red onion: 1 tablespoon, finely chopped

Fresh parsley or cilantro: 1 tablespoon, chopped

Olive oil: 1 teaspoon

Lime juice: 1 tablespoon

Salt: to taste

Black pepper: to taste

Procedure :

- Cook the Quinoa:

Rinse the quinoa under cold water.

In a small saucepan, bring 1/2 cup of water to a boil.

Add the quinoa, reduce the heat to low, cover, and simmer for 12-15 minutes, or until the water is absorbed and the quinoa is tender. Fluff with a fork and let it cool.

- Prepare the Vegetables:

Dice the avocado, cucumber, and red onion. Halve the cherry tomatoes. Chop the parsley or cilantro.

- Combine the Ingredients:

In a mixing bowl, combine the cooled quinoa, avocado, cherry tomatoes, cucumber, red onion, and parsley or cilantro.

- Dress the Salad.
- Serve.

Nutritions

Calories per Serving: 300 kcal

Protein: 6 g

Fat: 14 g

Carbohydrates: 36 g

Prep Time	:	10 min
Cook Time	:	15 min
Servings	:	1 serving

Salad with barley and tomatoes

Ingredients :

Pearl barley: 1/4 cup (dry)

Cherry tomatoes: 6-7, halved

Cucumber: 1/4, diced

Red onion: 1 tablespoon, finely chopped

Fresh parsley: 1 tablespoon, chopped

Olive oil: 1 teaspoon

Lemon juice or balsamic vinegar: 1
tablespoon

Salt: to taste

Black pepper: to taste

Optional topping: 1 teaspoon crumbled
feta or toasted sunflower seeds

Procedure :

- Cook the Barley:

Rinse the pearl barley under cold water.
In a small saucepan, bring 3/4 cup of water
to a boil.
Add the barley, reduce the heat to low,
and simmer for 25-30 minutes, or until
tender. Drain any excess water and let it
cool.

- Prepare the Vegetables:

Dice the cucumber, halve the cherry
tomatoes, and chop the parsley. Finely
chop the red onion.

- Combine the Ingredients:

In a large bowl, mix the cooked barley,
cherry tomatoes, cucumber, red onion,
and parsley.

- Dress the Salad.

- Serve.

Nutritions

Calories per Serving: 220 kcal

Protein: 5 g

Fat: 5 g

Carbohydrates: 40 g

Prep Time	:	10 min
Cook Time	:	30 min
Servings	:	1 serving

Pasta and Tuna Salad

Ingredients :

Pasta (any short variety, e.g., penne, fusilli): 1/2 cup (dry)

Canned tuna in water or oil: 1 small can (3 oz), drained

Cherry tomatoes: 5-6, halved

Cucumber: 1/4, diced

Red onion: 1 tablespoon, finely chopped

Fresh parsley or basil: 1 tablespoon, chopped

Olive oil: 1 teaspoon

Lemon juice: 1 tablespoon

Salt: to taste

Black pepper: to taste

Optional add-ins: 1 tablespoon sweet corn or diced olives

Procedure :

- Cook the Pasta:

Bring a small pot of salted water to a boil. Add the pasta and cook according to the package instructions (usually 8-10 minutes).

Drain the pasta, rinse under cold water to cool, and let it drain completely.

- Prepare the Ingredients:

Dice the cucumber, halve the cherry tomatoes, chop the red onion, and parsley or basil. Drain the tuna and flake it into smaller pieces.

- Combine the Ingredients.
- Dress the Salad.
- Serve.

Nutritions

Calories per Serving: 320 kcal

Protein: 20 g

Fat: 7 g

Carbohydrates: 42 g

Prep Time	:	10 min
Cook Time	:	10 min
Servings	:	1 serving

Salad with couscous and vegetables

Ingredients :

Couscous: 1/4 cup (dry)

Boiling water: 1/4 cup

Cherry tomatoes: 5-6, halved

Cucumber: 1/4, diced

Bell pepper (any color): 1/4, diced

Red onion: 1 tablespoon, finely chopped

Fresh parsley or cilantro: 1 tablespoon, chopped

Olive oil: 1 teaspoon

Lemon juice: 1 tablespoon

Salt: to taste

Black pepper: to taste

Optional topping: 1 teaspoon crumbled feta or toasted pine nuts

Procedure :

- Prepare the Couscous:

Place the couscous in a bowl and pour boiling water over it.

Cover with a plate and let it sit for 5 minutes.

Fluff with a fork to separate the grains and let it cool.

- Prepare the Vegetables:

Dice the cucumber and bell pepper, halve the cherry tomatoes, and chop the red onion and parsley or cilantro.

- Combine the Ingredients:

In a mixing bowl, combine the couscous, cherry tomatoes, cucumber, bell pepper, red onion, and parsley or cilantro.

- Dress the Salad.
- Serve:

Transfer to a serving plate or bowl and enjoy fresh or chilled.

Nutritions

Calories per Serving: 220 kcal

Protein: 5 g

Fat: 6 g

Carbohydrates: 35 g

Prep Time	:	**10 min**
Cook Time	:	**5 min**
Servings	:	**1 serving**

Quinoa and Black Bean Salad

Ingredients :

Quinoa: 1/4 cup (dry)

Black beans (canned or cooked): 1/3 cup, drained and rinsed

Cherry tomatoes: 5-6, halved

Cucumber: 1/4, diced

Red onion: 1 tablespoon, finely chopped

Corn kernels (optional): 2 tablespoons

Fresh cilantro or parsley: 1 tablespoon, chopped

Olive oil: 1 teaspoon

Lime juice: 1 tablespoon

Salt: to taste

Black pepper: to taste

Ground cumin (optional): 1/4 teaspoon

Procedure :

• Cook the Quinoa:

Rinse the quinoa under cold water.

In a small saucepan, bring 1/2 cup of water to a boil.

Add the quinoa, reduce the heat to low, cover, and simmer for 12-15 minutes, or until the quinoa is tender and the water is absorbed. Fluff with a fork and let it cool.

• Prepare the Vegetables:

Dice the cucumber, halve the cherry tomatoes, and chop the red onion and cilantro (or parsley).

• Combine the Ingredients:

In a large mixing bowl, combine the cooked quinoa, black beans, cherry tomatoes, cucumber, red onion, and corn (if using).

• Dress the Salad.

• Serve.

Nutritions

Calories per Serving: 300 kcal

Protein: 12 g

Fat: 7 g

Carbohydrates: 45 g

Prep Time : 10 min

Cook Time : 15 min

Servings : 1 serving

Pasta and spinach salad

Ingredients :

Pasta (short variety like penne, fusilli, or farfalle): 1/2 cup (dry)

Fresh spinach leaves: 1 cup

Cherry tomatoes: 5-6, halved

Cucumber: 1/4, diced

Red onion: 1 tablespoon, finely chopped

Feta cheese (optional): 1 tablespoon, crumbled

Olive oil: 1 teaspoon

Balsamic vinegar or lemon juice: 1 tablespoon

Salt: to taste

Black pepper: to taste

Garlic (optional): 1 small clove, minced

Procedure :

- Cook the Pasta:

Bring a small pot of salted water to a boil.

Add the pasta and cook according to the package instructions (usually 8-10 minutes).

Drain the pasta, rinse under cold water to cool, and let it drain completely.

- Prepare the Vegetables:

Wash the spinach leaves and pat dry.

Dice the cucumber, halve the cherry tomatoes, and chop the red onion.

If using garlic, mince it.

- Combine the Ingredients:

In a mixing bowl, combine the cooked pasta, spinach, cherry tomatoes, cucumber, red onion, and feta (if using).

- Dress the Salad.
- Serve.

Nutritions

Calories per Serving: 280 kcal

Protein: 8 g

Fat: 9 g

Carbohydrates: 38 g

Prep Time	:	10 min
Cook Time	:	10 min
Servings	:	1 serving

Chapter 5

Bean Salads

Hearty and Nutritious

Combining a variety of beans—such as black beans, kidney beans, chickpeas, or green beans—with fresh vegetables and flavorful dressings, these salads offer a satisfying mix of textures and tastes. Whether served as a side or a main dish, bean salads are versatile, easy to make, and packed with protein and fiber. Customize them with your favorite herbs, spices, and toppings for a healthy and vibrant addition to any meal.

Salad with beans and corn

Ingredients :

Canned beans (black beans, kidney beans, or chickpeas): 1/4 cup, drained and rinsed

Canned corn: 1/4 cup, drained

Cherry tomatoes: 5-6, halved

Cucumber: 1/4, diced

Red onion: 1 tablespoon, finely chopped

Fresh cilantro or parsley: 1 tablespoon, chopped

Olive oil: 1 teaspoon

Lime juice: 1 tablespoon

Salt: to taste

Black pepper: to taste

Optional spices: 1/4 teaspoon chili powder or cumin for extra flavor

Procedure :

- Prepare the Ingredients:

Drain and rinse the canned beans and corn.

Dice the cucumber, halve the cherry tomatoes, and chop the red onion and cilantro or parsley.

- Combine the Ingredients:

In a large bowl, mix the beans, corn, cherry tomatoes, cucumber, red onion, and cilantro (or parsley).

- Dress the Salad:

Drizzle with olive oil and lime juice. Season with salt, black pepper, and optional chili powder or cumin for extra flavor. Toss gently to combine.

- Serve:

Transfer to a serving plate or bowl and enjoy fresh.

Nutritions

Calories per Serving: 220 kcal

Protein: 7 g

Fat: 6 g

Carbohydrates: 35 g

Prep Time	:	10 min
Cook Time	:	10 min
Servings	:	1 serving

Chickpea and Tomato Salad

Ingredients :

Canned chickpeas: 1/4 cup, drained and rinsed

Cherry tomatoes: 6-7, halved

Cucumber: 1/4, diced

Red onion: 1 tablespoon, finely chopped

Fresh parsley or basil: 1 tablespoon, chopped

Olive oil: 1 teaspoon

Lemon juice: 1 tablespoon

Salt: to taste

Black pepper: to taste

Optional: 1 teaspoon crumbled feta or olives for extra flavor

Procedure :

- Prepare the Ingredients:

Drain and rinse the canned chickpeas.

Halve the cherry tomatoes and dice the cucumber.

Chop the red onion and parsley or basil.

- Combine the Ingredients:

In a large bowl, combine the chickpeas, cherry tomatoes, cucumber, red onion, and parsley (or basil).

- Dress the Salad:

Drizzle the salad with olive oil and lemon juice.

Season with salt and black pepper to taste.

Toss gently to combine.

- Serve:

Top with optional feta or olives for added flavor. Serve immediately or chill for later.

Nutritions

Calories per Serving: 250 kcal

Protein: 9 g

Fat: 9 g

Carbohydrates: 35 g

Prep Time : 10 min

Cook Time : 10 min

Servings : 1 serving

Lentil and Herb Salad

Ingredients :

Cooked lentils: 1/2 cup (canned or pre-cooked)

Cucumber: 1/4, diced

Cherry tomatoes: 5-6, halved

Red onion: 1 tablespoon, finely chopped

Fresh parsley: 1 tablespoon, chopped

Fresh mint (optional): 1 teaspoon, chopped

Olive oil: 1 teaspoon

Lemon juice: 1 tablespoon

Salt: to taste

Black pepper: to taste

Optional add-ins: 1 teaspoon crumbled feta or olives for extra flavor

Procedure :

• Prepare the Ingredients:

If using canned lentils, drain and rinse them. If cooking lentils from dry, rinse 1/4 cup dry lentils and cook in about 1/2 cup water for 15-20 minutes, or until tender. Drain and let them cool.

Dice the cucumber, halve the cherry tomatoes, chop the red onion, parsley, and optional mint.

• Combine the Ingredients:

In a mixing bowl, combine the cooked lentils, cucumber, cherry tomatoes, red onion, parsley, and mint.

• Dress the Salad:

Drizzle olive oil and lemon juice over the salad.

Season with salt and black pepper to taste. Toss gently to combine.

• Serve.

Nutritions

Calories per Serving: 250 kcal

Protein: 13 g

Fat: 7 g

Carbohydrates: 35 g

Prep Time	:	**10 min**
Cook Time	:	**20 min**
Servings	:	**1 serving**

Black Bean and Avocado Salad

Ingredients :

Canned black beans: 1/4 cup, drained and rinsed

Avocado: 1/2, diced

Cherry tomatoes: 5-6, halved

Red onion: 1 tablespoon, finely chopped

Cilantro or parsley: 1 tablespoon, chopped

Lime juice: 1 tablespoon

Olive oil: 1 teaspoon

Salt: to taste

Black pepper: to taste

Optional add-ins: 1 tablespoon corn kernels or a pinch of chili powder for extra flavor

Nutritions

Calories per Serving: 300 kcal

Protein: 9 g

Fat: 17 g

Carbohydrates: 32 g

Procedure :

- Prepare the Ingredients:

Drain and rinse the black beans.

Dice the avocado, halve the cherry tomatoes, chop the red onion, and cilantro (or parsley).

- Combine the Ingredients:

In a large mixing bowl, combine the black beans, avocado, cherry tomatoes, red onion, and cilantro (or parsley).

- Dress the Salad:

Drizzle olive oil and lime juice over the mixture.

Season with salt and black pepper to taste.

Toss gently to combine, making sure not to mash the avocado.

- Serve:

Add optional corn or a pinch of chili powder if desired. Serve immediately or chill before serving.

Prep Time	:	10 min
Cook Time	:	10 min
Servings	:	1 serving

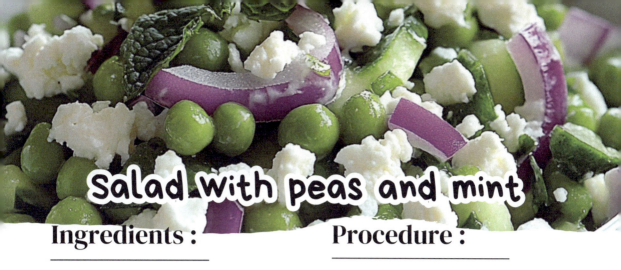

Salad with peas and mint

Ingredients :

Frozen peas: 1/2 cup

Fresh mint leaves: 1 tablespoon, chopped

Cucumber: 1/4, diced

Red onion: 1 tablespoon, finely chopped

Olive oil: 1 teaspoon

Lemon juice: 1 tablespoon

Salt: to taste

Black pepper: to taste

Optional add-ins: 1 teaspoon feta cheese or crumbled goat cheese for extra flavor

Procedure :

- Cook the Peas:

If using frozen peas, bring a small pot of water to a boil.

Add the peas and cook for about 2-3 minutes, or until tender. Drain and rinse under cold water to cool quickly.

- Prepare the Vegetables:

Dice the cucumber and chop the red onion and fresh mint leaves.

- Combine the Ingredients:

In a bowl, combine the cooled peas, diced cucumber, red onion, and chopped mint.

- Dress the Salad:

Drizzle with olive oil and lemon juice. Season with salt and black pepper to taste. Toss gently to combine.

- Serve.

Nutritions

Calories per Serving: 180 kcal

Protein: 6 g

Fat: 9 g

Carbohydrates: 23 g

Prep Time :	5 min
Cook Time :	3 min
Servings :	1 serving

Salad with beans and peppers

Ingredients :

Canned beans (black beans, kidney beans, or chickpeas): 1/4 cup, drained and rinsed

Bell pepper (any color): 1/4, diced

Cherry tomatoes: 5-6, halved

Red onion: 1 tablespoon, finely chopped

Olive oil: 1 teaspoon

Lime juice: 1 tablespoon

Salt: to taste

Black pepper: to taste

Fresh cilantro or parsley: 1 tablespoon, chopped

Optional add-ins: 1 teaspoon crumbled feta or a pinch of chili flakes for extra flavor

Procedure :

- Prepare the Ingredients:

Drain and rinse the canned beans.

Dice the bell pepper and chop the red onion and cilantro (or parsley).

Halve the cherry tomatoes.

- Combine the Ingredients:

In a bowl, mix the beans, bell pepper, cherry tomatoes, red onion, and cilantro (or parsley).

- Dress the Salad:

Drizzle with olive oil and lime juice.

Season with salt and black pepper to taste.

Toss gently to combine.

- Serve:

Optionally, top with crumbled feta or chili flakes for an extra burst of flavor. Serve immediately or chill before serving.

Nutritions

Calories per Serving: 230 kcal

Protein: 9 g

Fat: 8 g

Carbohydrates: 30 g

Prep Time : 10 min

Cook Time : 10 min

Servings : 1 serving

Salad with red lentils and spinach

Ingredients :

Red lentils (cooked): 1/4 cup (about 3-4 tablespoons dry)

Fresh spinach: 1 cup, washed and chopped

Cherry tomatoes: 5-6, halved

Cucumber: 1/4, diced

Red onion: 1 tablespoon, finely chopped

Olive oil: 1 teaspoon

Lemon juice: 1 tablespoon

Salt: to taste

Black pepper: to taste

Optional add-ins: 1 teaspoon crumbled feta or a sprinkle of sunflower seeds

Procedure :

- Cook the Lentils:

Rinse the red lentils under cold water. Cook in a small pot with 1/2 cup of water for about 10-12 minutes, or until tender. Drain any excess water and set aside to cool.

- Prepare the Vegetables:

Dice the cucumber, halve the cherry tomatoes, and finely chop the red onion. Wash and chop the spinach leaves.

- Combine the Ingredients:

In a large bowl, combine the cooked lentils, spinach, cherry tomatoes, cucumber, and red onion.

- Dress the Salad.

- Serve.

Nutritions

Calories per Serving: 250 kcal

Protein: 13 g

Fat: 8 g

Carbohydrates: 30 g

Prep Time : 10 min

Cook Time : 12 min

Servings : 1 serving

White Bean and Tuna Salad

Ingredients :

Canned white beans (such as cannellini or navy beans): 1/4 cup, drained and rinsed

Canned tuna in water or oil: 1 small can (3 oz), drained

Cherry tomatoes: 5-6, halved

Cucumber: 1/4, diced

Red onion: 1 tablespoon, finely chopped

Olive oil: 1 teaspoon

Lemon juice: 1 tablespoon

Salt: to taste

Black pepper: to taste

Fresh parsley or basil: 1 tablespoon, chopped

Optional add-ins: 1 teaspoon capers or olives for extra flavor

Procedure :

- Prepare the Ingredients:

Drain and rinse the white beans and tuna. Dice the cucumber, halve the cherry tomatoes, and chop the red onion and fresh herbs.

- Combine the Ingredients:

In a mixing bowl, combine the white beans, tuna, cherry tomatoes, cucumber, red onion, and fresh herbs.

- Dress the Salad:

Drizzle the olive oil and lemon juice over the mixture.

Season with salt and black pepper to taste. Toss gently to combine.

- Serve:

Optionally, add capers or olives for an extra burst of flavor. Serve immediately or chill for later.

Nutritions

Calories per Serving: 280 kcal

Protein: 25 g

Fat: 12 g

Carbohydrates: 18 g

Prep Time	:	**10 min**
Cook Time	:	**5 min**
Servings	:	**1 serving**

Salad with beans and lemon sauce

Ingredients :

Canned beans (such as black beans, kidney beans, or chickpeas): 1/4 cup, drained and rinsed

Cucumber: 1/4, diced

Cherry tomatoes: 5-6, halved

Red onion: 1 tablespoon, finely chopped

Fresh parsley or cilantro: 1 tablespoon, chopped

Olive oil: 1 teaspoon

Lemon juice: 1 tablespoon (for sauce)

Garlic: 1 small clove, minced

Salt: to taste

Black pepper: to taste

Water (for sauce): 1 teaspoon

Optional add-ins: 1 teaspoon crumbled feta or a pinch of chili flakes for extra flavor

Nutritions

Calories per Serving: 220 kcal

Protein: 30 g

Fat: 8 g

Carbohydrates: 30 g

Procedure :

- Prepare the Ingredients:

Drain and rinse the canned beans.

Dice the cucumber, halve the cherry tomatoes, and chop the red onion and fresh parsley (or cilantro).

Mince the garlic.

- Make the Lemon Sauce:

In a small bowl, whisk together the lemon juice, olive oil, minced garlic, water, salt, and black pepper. Adjust seasoning to taste.

- Combine the Salad.

- Dress the Salad:

Pour the lemon sauce over the salad and toss gently to combine.

- Serve:

Optionally, top with crumbled feta or a pinch of chili flakes for added flavor. Serve immediately or refrigerate for later.

Prep Time	:	10 min
Cook Time	:	5 min
Servings	:	1 serving

Chickpea and Sweet Potato Salad

Ingredients :

Canned chickpeas: 1/4 cup, drained and rinsed

Sweet potato: 1 small, peeled and diced

Olive oil: 1 teaspoon (for roasting sweet potato)

Cherry tomatoes: 5-6, halved

Spinach or mixed greens: 1 cup

Red onion: 1 tablespoon, finely chopped

Lemon juice: 1 tablespoon

Tahini: 1 teaspoon (optional for dressing)

Salt: to taste

Black pepper: to taste

Cumin or smoked paprika (optional): 1/4 teaspoon for extra flavor

Procedure :

- Roast the Sweet Potato:

Preheat your oven to 400°F (200°C).

Toss the diced sweet potato with olive oil, salt, and pepper, and optional cumin or paprika.

Spread the sweet potato on a baking sheet in a single layer.

Roast for 20-25 minutes, flipping halfway, until the sweet potato is tender and slightly browned. Remove from the oven and let cool.

- Prepare the Ingredients.
- Make the Dressing.

In a small bowl, whisk together lemon juice, tahini (if using), a pinch of salt, and black pepper. Adjust consistency with a splash of water if needed.

- Assemble the Salad.
- Dress the Salad:

Drizzle the tahini lemon dressing over the salad and toss gently to combine.

- Serve.

Nutritions

Calories per Serving: 350 kcal

Protein: 12 g

Fat: 12 g

Carbohydrates: 50 g

Prep Time	:	10 min
Cook Time	:	20-25 min
Servings	:	1 serving

Chapter 6

Fruit Salads

Refreshing and Colorful

Fruit salads are refreshing dishes that celebrate the natural sweetness of fresh fruits. Perfect for breakfasts, desserts, or light snacks, they can be as simple or elaborate as you like. A mix of seasonal fruits, combined with a hint of citrus, honey, or mint, creates a delightful balance of flavors. Easy to prepare and endlessly versatile, fruit salads are a crowd-pleasing way to enjoy nature's finest ingredients.

Salad with watermelon and feta

Ingredients :

Watermelon: 1 cup, diced

Feta cheese: 1/4 cup, crumbled

Cucumber: 1/4, sliced or diced

Fresh mint leaves: 1 tablespoon, chopped

Olive oil: 1 teaspoon

Lime juice: 1 tablespoon

Salt: a pinch (optional)

Black pepper: to taste

Procedure :

- Prepare the Ingredients:

Dice the watermelon into bite-sized cubes.

Slice or dice the cucumber.

Chop the fresh mint leaves.

Crumble the feta cheese if not already crumbled.

- Assemble the Salad:

In a large bowl, combine the watermelon, cucumber, and mint leaves.

Add the crumbled feta cheese on top.

- Dress the Salad:

Drizzle with olive oil and lime juice.

Add a pinch of salt (optional) and season with black pepper to taste. Toss gently to combine.

- Serve:

Serve immediately for a refreshing, flavorful salad.

Nutritions

Calories per Serving: 200 kcal

Protein: 5 g

Fat: 10 g

Carbohydrates: 22 g

Prep Time	:	10 min
Cook Time	:	10 min
Servings	:	1 serving

Salad with mango and shrimps

Ingredients :

Shrimp (peeled and deveined): 3 oz
(about 6-8 medium shrimp)

Mango: 1/2, diced

Mixed greens or arugula: 1 cup

Cucumber: 1/4, sliced or diced

Red onion: 1 tablespoon, thinly sliced

Olive oil: 1 teaspoon (for cooking
shrimp)

Lime juice: 1 tablespoon

Olive oil (for dressing): 1 teaspoon

Salt: to taste

Black pepper: to taste

Optional add-ins: 1 teaspoon chopped
fresh cilantro or chili flakes for extra
flavor

Nutritions

Calories per Serving: 210 kcal

Protein: 18 g

Fat: 8 g

Carbohydrates: 17 g

Procedure :

- Cook the Shrimp:

Heat 1 teaspoon of olive oil in a skillet
over medium heat.

Season the shrimp with a pinch of salt and
black pepper.

Cook the shrimp for 2-3 minutes per side
until pink and opaque. Remove from heat
and let cool slightly.

- Prepare the Ingredients:

Dice the mango and cucumber.

Slice the red onion thinly.

Wash and dry the mixed greens or arugula.

- Make the Dressing:

In a small bowl, whisk together lime juice,
1 teaspoon olive oil, salt, and pepper.

Adjust seasoning as desired.

- Assemble the Salad.

- Dress the Salad.

- Serve.

Prep Time	:	10 min
Cook Time	:	5 min
Servings	:	1 serving

Salad with pear and nuts

Ingredients :

Fresh pear: 1 small, sliced

Mixed greens (e.g., arugula, spinach, or lettuce): 1 cup

Walnuts or pecans: 1 tablespoon, roughly chopped

Feta or goat cheese (optional): 1 tablespoon, crumbled

Olive oil: 1 teaspoon

Balsamic vinegar: 1 teaspoon

Honey: 1/2 teaspoon (optional, for sweetness)

Salt: a pinch

Black pepper: to taste

Procedure :

- Prepare the Ingredients:
Wash and slice the pear thinly.
Roughly chop the nuts.
Wash and dry the mixed greens.

- Toast the Nuts (Optional):
In a dry skillet over medium heat, toast the nuts for 2-3 minutes, stirring frequently, until fragrant. Let cool slightly.

- Make the Dressing:
In a small bowl, whisk together olive oil, balsamic vinegar, honey (if using), salt, and pepper.

- Assemble the Salad.

- Dress the Salad:
Drizzle the balsamic dressing over the salad. Toss gently to combine.

- Serve.

Nutritions

Calories per Serving: 200 kcal

Protein: 4 g

Fat: 12 g

Carbohydrates: 21 g

Prep Time	:	8 min
Cook Time	:	2-3 min
Servings	:	1 serving

Classic Rainbow Fruit Salad

Ingredients :

Strawberries (hulled and sliced): 1/4 cup

Blueberries: 1/4 cup

Kiwi (peeled and diced): 1/4 cup

Pineapple (diced): 1/4 cup

Grapes (halved): 1/4 cup

Fresh orange juice: 2 tablespoons

Lime zest: 1/4 teaspoon

Procedure :

- Prepare the Fruit:

Wash and prepare the strawberries, blueberries, kiwi, pineapple, and grapes as specified. Place them in a medium-sized bowl.

- Make the Dressing:

In a small bowl, mix the orange juice and lime zest until well combined.

- Combine:

Pour the dressing over the fruit mixture and gently toss to coat evenly.

- Serve:

Transfer the fruit salad to a serving bowl and enjoy immediately for the freshest taste.

Nutritions

Calories per Serving: 1100 kcal

Protein: 1.5 g

Fat: 0.5 g

Carbohydrates: 27 g

Prep Time : 10 min

Cook Time : 10 min

Servings : 1 serving

Strawberry and Spinach Salad

Ingredients :

Fresh spinach: 1 cup, washed and dried

Strawberries: 1/2 cup, hulled and sliced

Feta cheese (optional): 1 tablespoon, crumbled

Walnuts or pecans: 1 tablespoon, roughly chopped

Red onion: 1 tablespoon, thinly sliced

Olive oil: 1 teaspoon

Balsamic vinegar: 1 teaspoon

Honey: 1/2 teaspoon

Salt: a pinch

Black pepper: to taste

Procedure :

- Prepare the Ingredients:

Wash and dry the spinach leaves.

Hull and slice the strawberries.

Thinly slice the red onion.

Roughly chop the walnuts or pecans.

- Toast the Nuts (Optional):

In a dry skillet over medium heat, toast the walnuts or pecans for 2-3 minutes until fragrant. Let cool.

- Make the Dressing:

In a small bowl, whisk together olive oil, balsamic vinegar, honey, salt, and black pepper.

- Assemble the Salad.

- Dress the Salad:

Drizzle the balsamic dressing over the salad. Toss gently to combine.

- Serve.

Nutritions

Calories per Serving: 180 kcal

Protein: 4 g

Fat: 10 g

Carbohydrates: 18 g

Prep Time	:	8 min
Cook Time	:	2-3 min
Servings	:	1 serving

Salad with oranges and avocado

Ingredients :

Fresh orange: 1 medium, peeled and segmented

Avocado: 1/2, sliced

Mixed greens (e.g., arugula, spinach, or lettuce): 1 cup

Red onion: 1 tablespoon, thinly sliced

Olive oil: 1 teaspoon

Lemon or lime juice: 1 teaspoon

Honey (optional): 1/2 teaspoon

Salt: a pinch

Black pepper: to taste

Optional garnish: 1 teaspoon toasted sesame seeds or chopped fresh mint

Procedure :

- Prepare the Ingredients:

Peel the orange and segment it, removing any seeds.

Slice the avocado.

Thinly slice the red onion.

Wash and dry the mixed greens.

- Make the Dressing:

In a small bowl, whisk together olive oil, lemon or lime juice, honey (if using), salt, and black pepper.

- Assemble the Salad:

Arrange the mixed greens on a plate or in a bowl as a base.

Add the orange segments, avocado slices, and red onion on top.

- Dress the Salad:

Drizzle the dressing over the salad. Toss gently to combine.

- Serve.

Nutritions

Calories per Serving: 210 kcal

Protein: 2 g

Fat: 14 g

Carbohydrates: 20 g

Prep Time	:	2 min
Cook Time	:	10 min
Servings	:	1 serving

Salad with peaches and mozzarella

Ingredients :

Fresh peach: 1 medium, sliced

Mozzarella (fresh, small ball or sliced): 1 oz (about 1/4 cup)

Arugula or mixed greens: 1 cup

Basil leaves: 2-3, torn or chopped

Olive oil: 1 teaspoon

Balsamic glaze (optional): 1/2 teaspoon

Salt: a pinch

Black pepper: to taste

Optional garnish: 1 teaspoon chopped nuts (e.g., almonds, walnuts)

Procedure :

- Prepare the Ingredients:

Wash and slice the peach into thin wedges.

Slice the mozzarella if not already prepared.

Tear or chop the fresh basil leaves.

Wash and dry the arugula or mixed greens.

- Make the Salad Base:

Arrange the arugula or mixed greens on a serving plate or bowl.

- Assemble the Salad:

Place the peach slices and mozzarella over the greens.

Sprinkle the torn basil leaves over the top.

- Dress the Salad:

Optionally, sprinkle with chopped nuts for extra crunch.

- Serve.

Nutritions

Calories per Serving: 180 kcal

Protein: 6 g

Fat: 10 g

Carbohydrates: 15 g

Prep Time :	8 min
Cook Time :	10 min
Servings :	1 serving

Salad with apples and celery

Ingredients :

Apple (any crisp variety, e.g., Granny Smith or Fuji): 1 small, diced

Celery: 1 stalk, thinly sliced

Walnuts (optional): 1 tablespoon, roughly chopped

Greek yogurt or mayonnaise (for dressing): 1 tablespoon

Lemon juice: 1 teaspoon

Honey (optional): 1/2 teaspoon

Salt: a pinch

Black pepper: to taste

Optional garnish: 1 teaspoon raisins or dried cranberries

Procedure :

- Prepare the Ingredients:

Wash and dice the apple into bite-sized pieces.

Thinly slice the celery.

Roughly chop the walnuts, if using.

- Make the Dressing:

In a small bowl, mix Greek yogurt or mayonnaise with lemon juice, honey (if using), salt, and black pepper.

- Assemble the Salad:

In a mixing bowl, combine the diced apple, celery, and walnuts (optional). Add the dressing and toss to coat evenly.

- Plate the Salad.
- Serve:

Serve immediately as a crisp and refreshing salad.

Nutritions

Calories per Serving: 160 kcal

Protein: 3 g

Fat: 7 g

Carbohydrates: 22 g

Prep Time :	**8 min**
Cook Time :	**8 min**
Servings :	**1 serving**

Salad with kiwi and mint

Ingredients :

Kiwi: 2, peeled and sliced

Fresh mint leaves: 1 tablespoon, chopped

Arugula or mixed greens: 1 cup

Honey (optional): 1 teaspoon

Lime juice: 1 teaspoon

Olive oil: 1 teaspoon

Salt: a pinch

Black pepper: to taste

Optional garnish: 1 teaspoon chia seeds
or crushed pistachios

Procedure :

- Prepare the Ingredients:

Peel and slice the kiwi into rounds or half-moons.

Chop the fresh mint leaves.

Wash and dry the arugula or mixed greens.

- Make the Dressing:

In a small bowl, whisk together lime juice, olive oil, honey (if using), salt, and black pepper.

- Assemble the Salad:

Arrange the arugula or mixed greens on a serving plate.

Top with sliced kiwi and chopped mint.

- Dress the Salad:

Drizzle the lime dressing over the salad.

Toss gently to combine.

- Garnish and Serve.

Nutritions

Calories per Serving: 120 kcal

Protein: 2 g

Fat: 4 g

Carbohydrates: 20 g

Prep Time	:	8 min
Cook Time	:	10 min
Servings	:	1 serving

Salad with berries and yogurt

Ingredients :

Mixed berries (e.g., strawberries, blueberries, raspberries): 1/2 cup

Greek yogurt (plain, unsweetened): 1/2 cup

Honey (optional): 1 teaspoon

Chia seeds or flaxseeds (optional): 1 teaspoon

Mint leaves (optional): 1-2, chopped

Almonds or walnuts (optional): 1 tablespoon, chopped

Procedure :

- Prepare the Ingredients:

Wash and dry the mixed berries.

Chop mint leaves and nuts (if using).

- Assemble the Salad:

In a serving bowl, add the mixed berries.

Top with Greek yogurt.

Drizzle with honey, if desired.

- Add Optional Toppings:

Sprinkle chia seeds or flaxseeds on top for added texture and nutrition.

Garnish with chopped mint leaves and nuts for extra crunch and flavor.

- Serve:

Serve immediately as a refreshing and healthy fruit salad.

Nutritions

Calories per Serving: 180 kcal

Protein: 12 g

Fat: 7 g

Carbohydrates: 20 g

Prep Time :	**5 min**
Cook Time :	**10 min**
Servings :	**1 serving**

Chapter 7

Special Occasion Salads

The Perfect Way to Elevate any Celebration

Unique occasion salads with vibrant colors, elegant flavors, and fresh ingredients. These salads often feature a mix of greens, fruits, nuts, cheeses, and gourmet dressings, making them as visually stunning as they are delicious. Whether served as a side or a main course, unique occasion salads are designed to impress, combining seasonal produce and unique combinations for a memorable dining experience. Perfect for holidays, dinner parties, or any milestone event, these salads bring sophistication and freshness to your table.

Salad with duck and cherry

Ingredients :

Duck breast (cooked, skin on or off, as preferred): 4 oz

Fresh cherries (pitted and halved): 1/2 cup

Mixed greens (e.g., arugula, spinach, or baby kale): 1 cup

Red onion: 1 tablespoon, thinly sliced

Goat cheese or feta (optional): 1 tablespoon, crumbled

Olive oil: 1 teaspoon

Balsamic vinegar or cherry balsamic vinegar (optional): 1 teaspoon

Honey (optional): 1/2 teaspoon

Salt and black pepper: to taste

Chopped fresh herbs (e.g., thyme or mint): 1 teaspoon

Procedure :

- Prepare the Duck:

If not already cooked, pan-sear or roast the duck breast until the internal temperature reaches 135°F (57°C) for medium-rare, or cook to your preferred doneness. Let it rest for 5 minutes before slicing into thin strips.

If using leftover duck, simply slice it into thin strips.

- Prepare the Ingredients:

Pit and halve the cherries.

Wash and dry the mixed greens and thinly slice the red onion.

Crumble the goat cheese or feta, if using.

- Make the Dressing.

In a small bowl, whisk together olive oil, balsamic vinegar, honey (if using), a pinch of salt, and black pepper.

- Assemble the Salad.
- Dress the Salad.
- Garnish and Serve.

Nutritions

Calories per Serving: 350 kcal

Protein: 24 g

Fat: 2 g

Carbohydrates: 15 g

Prep Time	:	10 min
Cook Time	:	15-20 min
Servings	:	1 serving

Caprese-Style Salad with a Twist

Ingredients :

Cherry tomatoes (halved): 1/2 cup

Fresh mozzarella balls (bocconcini): 1/4 cup

Fresh basil leaves: 5-6 leaves

Avocado (diced): 1/4 medium

Balsamic glaze: 1 teaspoon

Extra virgin olive oil: 1 teaspoon

Salt: To taste

Freshly cracked black pepper: To taste

Procedure :

- Prepare the Ingredients:

Wash and halve the cherry tomatoes.

Dice the avocado and drain the mozzarella balls.

- Assemble the Salad:

Arrange the cherry tomatoes, mozzarella balls, diced avocado, and basil leaves on a plate or in a bowl.

- Drizzle and Season:

Drizzle the balsamic glaze and olive oil over the salad.

Sprinkle with salt and freshly cracked black pepper to taste.

- Serve:

Serve immediately and enjoy this fresh twist on a classic Caprese salad!

Nutritions

Calories per Serving: 200 kcal

Protein: 8 g

Fat: 15 g

Carbohydrates: 7 g

Prep Time :	**10 min**
Cook Time :	**10 min**
Servings :	**1 serving**

Crab and Mango Party Salad

Ingredients :

Cooked crab meat (fresh or canned): 3 oz

Ripe mango: 1/2, peeled and diced

Mixed greens (e.g., arugula, spinach, or baby kale): 1 cup

Cucumber: 1/4, thinly sliced

Cherry tomatoes: 1/4 cup, halved

Red onion: 1 tablespoon, thinly sliced

Avocado: 1/4, sliced

Olive oil: 1 teaspoon

Lime juice: 1 tablespoon (freshly squeezed)

Honey (optional): 1/2 teaspoon

Fresh cilantro (optional): 1 teaspoon, chopped

Salt and black pepper: to taste

Pomegranate seeds (for garnish, optional): 1 tablespoon

Procedure :

- Prepare the Crab:

If using canned crab meat, drain and gently rinse to remove any excess liquid. If using fresh crab, shred or flake the meat into bite-sized pieces. Set aside.

- Prepare the Vegetables and Mango:

Peel and dice the mango into small cubes. Slice the cucumber and red onion thinly, and halve the cherry tomatoes. Slice the avocado into wedges.

- Make the Dressing:

In a small bowl, whisk together lime juice, olive oil, honey (if using), salt, and black pepper to taste.

- Assemble the Salad.
- Dress the Salad.
- Garnish and Serve.

Nutritions

Calories per Serving: 280 kcal

Protein: 20 g

Fat: 16 g

Carbohydrates: 20 g

Prep Time : 10 min

Cook Time : 10 min

Servings : 1 serving

Salad with beef and truffle oil

Ingredients :

Beef steak (e.g., sirloin or ribeye): 4 oz (cooked to desired doneness, sliced thinly)

Mixed greens (e.g., arugula, baby spinach, or frisée): 2 cups

Cherry tomatoes: 1/4 cup, halved

Cucumber: 1/4, thinly sliced

Red onion: 1 tablespoon, thinly sliced

Parmesan cheese (optional): 1 tablespoon, shaved or grated

Truffle oil: 1 teaspoon

Balsamic vinegar (optional): 1 teaspoon

Olive oil: 1 teaspoon

Salt and black pepper: to taste

Fresh herbs (optional, e.g., parsley or thyme): 1 teaspoon, chopped

Nutritions

Calories per Serving: 350 kcal

Protein: 28 g

Fat: 24 g

Carbohydrates: 6 g

Procedure :

- Cook the Beef:

Season the beef steak with salt and black pepper.

Heat a small pan over medium-high heat and cook the steak to your preferred doneness (about 3-4 minutes per side for medium-rare).

Once cooked, remove the steak from the pan and let it rest for 5 minutes.

Slice the beef thinly against the grain.

- Prepare the Vegetables:
- Slice the cucumber and halve the cherry tomatoes. Thinly slice the red onion.
- Make the Dressing.

In a small bowl, whisk together truffle oil, olive oil, balsamic vinegar (if using), and a pinch of salt and black pepper.

- Assemble the Salad.
- Dress the Salad:.
- Garnish and Serve.

Prep Time	:	10 min
Cook Time	:	10 min
Servings	:	1 serving

Salad with goat cheese and figs

Ingredients :

Goat cheese (crumbled or in small rounds): 2 oz

Fresh figs: 2-3, halved or quartered

Mixed greens (e.g., arugula, spinach, or baby kale): 2 cups

Walnuts or pecans (optional): 1 tablespoon, chopped

Red onion: 1 tablespoon, thinly sliced

Balsamic glaze or vinegar: 1 tablespoon

Olive oil: 1 teaspoon

Honey (optional): 1 teaspoon

Salt and black pepper: to taste

Fresh herbs (optional, e.g., thyme or basil): 1 teaspoon, chopped

Procedure :

- Prepare the Figs:
Wash and halve or quarter the fresh figs. Set aside.

- Prepare the Greens:
Wash and dry the mixed greens. Place them in a bowl or on a plate.

- Toast the Nuts (optional):
If using walnuts or pecans, toast them in a dry pan over medium heat for 2-3 minutes until fragrant. Let them cool and chop them into smaller pieces.

- Assemble the Salad.

- Make the Dressing:
In a small bowl, whisk together the balsamic glaze or vinegar, olive oil, honey (if using), salt, and black pepper.

- Dress the Salad.

- Garnish and Serve.

Nutritions

Calories per Serving: 320 kcal

Protein: 9 g

Fat: 24 g

Carbohydrates: 25 g

Prep Time	:	10 min
Cook Time	:	2-3 min
Servings	:	1 serving

BBQ Chicken Pineapple Salad

Ingredients :

Chicken breast (boneless, skinless): 4 oz

Pineapple (fresh or canned, drained): 1/2 cup, diced

Mixed greens (e.g., arugula, spinach, or baby kale): 2 cups

Cherry tomatoes: 1/4 cup, halved

Red onion: 1 tablespoon, thinly sliced

Cucumber: 1/4, thinly sliced

BBQ sauce (low-sugar, if preferred): 2 tablespoons

Olive oil (for cooking): 1 teaspoon

Lime juice (optional): 1 teaspoon

Salt and black pepper: to taste

Fresh cilantro (optional): 1 teaspoon, chopped

Procedure :

- Prepare the Chicken:

Season the chicken breast with salt and black pepper.

Heat 1 teaspoon of olive oil in a non-stick pan over medium heat.

Cook the chicken breast for about 5-6 minutes per side, or until it reaches an internal temperature of 165°F (74°C).

Once cooked, remove the chicken from the pan and let it rest for a few minutes. Slice the chicken into strips.

- Prepare the Vegetables and Pineapple.
- Coat the Chicken with BBQ Sauce.
- Assemble the Salad.
- Dress the Salad.
- Garnish and Serve:

Garnish with fresh cilantro for a burst of freshness and color.

Serve immediately and enjoy!

Nutritions

Calories per Serving: 400 kcal

Protein: 32 g

Fat: 16 g

Carbohydrates: 35 g

Prep Time	:	10 min
Cook Time	:	10-12 min
Servings	:	1 serving

Seafood Salad with Lemon Sauce

Ingredients :

Mixed seafood (shrimp, scallops, and/or crab meat): 4 oz (use a combination of your favorite seafood)

Mixed greens (e.g., arugula, spinach, or baby kale): 2 cups

Cucumber: 1/4, thinly sliced

Cherry tomatoes: 1/4 cup, halved

Avocado: 1/4, sliced

Red onion: 1 tablespoon, thinly sliced

Olive oil: 1 teaspoon

Lemon (for juice and zest): 1/2 lemon

Garlic (optional): 1 small clove, minced

Dijon mustard (optional): 1/2 teaspoon

Fresh parsley (optional): 1 teaspoon, chopped

Salt and black pepper: to taste

Nutritions

Calories per Serving: 320 kcal

Protein: 30 g

Fat: 20 g

Carbohydrates: 12 g

Procedure :

- Prepare the Seafood:

If using shrimp, peel and devein them if necessary. For scallops, ensure they are clean and patted dry.

Heat 1 teaspoon of olive oil in a pan over medium-high heat.

Add the seafood to the pan, cooking shrimp for 2-3 minutes per side, and scallops for about 2 minutes per side until opaque and cooked through.

Season the seafood with salt, black pepper, and a squeeze of lemon juice. Set aside to cool slightly.

- Prepare the Salad Ingredients.
- Make the Lemon Dressing.

In a small bowl, whisk together the juice of 1/2 lemon, a pinch of lemon zest, olive oil, minced garlic (if using), Dijon mustard (if using), and a pinch of salt and black pepper. Adjust seasoning to taste.

- Assemble the Salad.
- Dress the Salad.
- Garnish and Serve.

Prep Time	:	10 min
Cook Time	:	10 min
Servings	:	1 serving

Roast Beef and Horseradish Salad

Ingredients :

Roast beef (thinly sliced, preferably from a roast or deli-style): 4 oz

Mixed greens (e.g., arugula, spinach, or baby kale): 2 cups

Cherry tomatoes: 1/4 cup, halved

Cucumber: 1/4, thinly sliced

Red onion: 1 tablespoon, thinly sliced

Avocado: 1/4, sliced

Fresh horseradish (or prepared horseradish): 1 teaspoon

Olive oil: 1 teaspoon

Balsamic vinegar (or red wine vinegar): 1 teaspoon

Dijon mustard: 1/2 teaspoon

Fresh parsley (optional): 1 teaspoon, chopped

Salt and black pepper: to taste

Nutritions

Calories per Serving: 320 kcal

Protein: 28 g

Fat: 22 g

Carbohydrates: 9 g

Procedure :

- Prepare the Roast Beef:

If not already pre-sliced, thinly slice the roast beef into strips or pieces. Set aside.

- Prepare the Salad Ingredients:

Wash and dry the mixed greens, then place them in a bowl or on a plate. Slice the cucumber, halve the cherry tomatoes, and thinly slice the red onion. Slice the avocado into thin wedges.

- Make the Horseradish Dressing:

In a small bowl, mix together the horseradish, olive oil, balsamic vinegar (or red wine vinegar), Dijon mustard, salt, and black pepper.

Whisk well to combine and create a creamy dressing.

- Assemble the Salad.
- Dress the Salad.
- Garnish and Serve.

Prep Time	:	10 min
Cook Time	:	10 min
Servings	:	1 serving

Smoked Salmon and Avocado Brunch

Ingredients :

Smoked salmon: 3 oz

Mixed greens (e.g., arugula, spinach, or baby kale): 2 cups

Avocado: 1/2, sliced

Cherry tomatoes: 1/4 cup, halved

Cucumber: 1/4, thinly sliced

Red onion: 1 tablespoon, thinly sliced

Lemon (for juice and zest): 1/2 lemon

Olive oil: 1 teaspoon

Dijon mustard: 1 teaspoon

Fresh dill (optional): 1 teaspoon, chopped

Capers (optional): 1 teaspoon

Salt and black pepper: to taste

Procedure :

- Prepare the Salad Ingredients:
Wash and dry the mixed greens, then place them in a bowl or on a plate. Slice the avocado into thin wedges. Halve the cherry tomatoes and slice the cucumber. Thinly slice the red onion.

- Prepare the Smoked Salmon:
Tear the smoked salmon into bite-sized pieces or leave it in larger slices, depending on preference.

- Make the Dressing:
In a small bowl, combine the juice of 1/2 lemon, Dijon mustard, olive oil, and a pinch of salt and black pepper. Whisk until the dressing emulsifies.

- Assemble the Salad.

- Dress the Salad.

- Garnish and Serve.

Nutritions

Calories per Serving: 350 kcal

Protein: 20 g

Fat: 26 g

Carbohydrates: 14 g

Prep Time	:	10 min
Cook Time	:	9 min
Servings	:	1 serving

Picnic Grilled Vegetable Salad

Ingredients :

Zucchini: 1/2, sliced

Red bell pepper: 1/2, sliced

Yellow bell pepper: 1/2, sliced

Eggplant: 1/4, sliced

Cherry tomatoes: 1/4 cup

Red onion: 1/4, sliced

Olive oil: 1 tablespoon

Balsamic vinegar: 1 teaspoon

Fresh basil or parsley (optional): 1
tablespoon, chopped

Garlic powder: 1/4 teaspoon

Dried oregano: 1/4 teaspoon

Salt and black pepper: to taste

Lemon (for zest and juice): 1/2 lemon

Procedure :

- Prepare the Vegetables.
- Grill the Vegetables:

Preheat a grill or grill pan over medium heat.

Toss the sliced vegetables (zucchini, bell peppers, eggplant, and red onion) with olive oil, garlic powder, dried oregano, salt, and pepper.

Grill the vegetables for 4-5 minutes on each side, or until they are tender and have nice grill marks. Grill the cherry tomatoes for about 2-3 minutes, turning them to avoid overcooking.

Remove from the grill and set aside to cool slightly.

- Make the Dressing.

In a small bowl, whisk together balsamic vinegar, a squeeze of lemon juice, and a pinch of lemon zest. Adjust seasoning with salt and black pepper to taste.

- Assemble the Salad.
- Garnish and Serve.

Nutritions

Calories per Serving: 200 kcal

Protein: 3 g

Fat: 14 g

Carbohydrates: 20 g

Prep Time	:	10 min
Cook Time	:	10-12 min
Servings	:	1 serving

Chapter 8

Nut and Seed Salads

Crunchy, Nutrient-Packed Addition to any Meal

These salads are full of wholesome ingredients like almonds, walnuts, sunflower seeds, and chia seeds, offering a satisfying blend of textures and flavors. Paired with fresh greens, vegetables, and a light dressing, nuts and seeds provide a rich source of protein, healthy fats, and essential vitamins. Nut and seed salads are perfect for adding extra crunch and nourishment to your diet, whether as a stand-alone dish or a topping for other salads.

Salad with walnuts and apples

Ingredients :

Mixed greens (e.g., arugula, spinach, or spring mix): 2 cups

Apple (crisp variety like Honeycrisp or Granny Smith): 1/2, thinly sliced

Walnuts: 2 tablespoons, roughly chopped

Dried cranberries (optional): 1 tablespoon

Feta or goat cheese (optional): 1 tablespoon, crumbled

Olive oil: 1 teaspoon

Apple cider vinegar: 1 teaspoon

Honey or maple syrup: 1/2 teaspoon

Dijon mustard (optional): 1/4 teaspoon

Salt and black pepper: to taste

Procedure :

- Prepare the Salad Base:
Wash and dry the mixed greens. Place them in a bowl or on a serving plate. Core and thinly slice the apple, leaving the skin on for added color and nutrients.

- Toast the Walnuts (Optional):
If desired, lightly toast the chopped walnuts in a dry skillet over medium heat for 2-3 minutes to enhance their flavor. Set aside to cool.

- Make the Dressing:
In a small bowl, whisk together olive oil, apple cider vinegar, honey (or maple syrup), Dijon mustard (if using), salt, and black pepper until emulsified. Adjust seasoning to taste.

- Assemble the Salad.

- Dress the Salad.

- Serve.

Nutritions

Calories per Serving: 220 kcal

Protein: 4 g

Fat: 14 g

Carbohydrates: 21 g

Prep Time :	10 min
Cook Time :	1-3 min
Servings :	1 serving

Cashew and Mango Salad

Ingredients :

Mixed greens (e.g., arugula, spinach, or lettuce): 2 cups

Fresh mango: 1/2, diced

Cashews (unsalted): 2 tablespoons, roughly chopped

Red bell pepper: 1/4, thinly sliced

Cucumber: 1/4, thinly sliced

Red onion: 1 tablespoon, thinly sliced

Fresh mint leaves (optional): 1 tablespoon, chopped

Olive oil: 1 teaspoon

Lime juice: 1 teaspoon

Honey or maple syrup: 1/2 teaspoon

Soy sauce (optional, for a savory note): 1/2 teaspoon

Salt and black pepper: to taste

Nutritions

Calories per Serving: 220 kcal

Protein: 4 g

Fat: 11 g

Carbohydrates: 27 g

Procedure :

- Prepare the Salad Ingredients:
Wash and dry the mixed greens. Place them in a bowl or on a serving plate. Peel and dice the mango. Thinly slice the red bell pepper, cucumber, and red onion.

- Toast the Cashews (Optional):
For added flavor, lightly toast the cashews in a dry skillet over medium heat for 2-3 minutes until golden and fragrant. Let cool.

- Make the Dressing:
In a small bowl, whisk together olive oil, lime juice, honey (or maple syrup), soy sauce (if using), and a pinch of salt and black pepper. Taste and adjust the flavors to balance sweetness and acidity.

- Assemble the Salad.
- Dress the Salad.
- Serve.

Prep Time	:	10 min
Cook Time	:	1-3 min
Servings	:	1 serving

Salad with Chia Seeds and Berries

Ingredients :

Mixed greens (e.g., spinach, arugula, or kale): 2 cups

Fresh berries (e.g., strawberries, blueberries, raspberries): 1/2 cup

Chia seeds: 1 teaspoon

Walnuts or almonds (optional): 1 tablespoon, roughly chopped

Feta or goat cheese (optional): 1 tablespoon, crumbled

Olive oil: 1 teaspoon

Balsamic vinegar: 1 teaspoon

Honey or maple syrup: 1/2 teaspoon

Lemon juice: 1/2 teaspoon

Salt and black pepper: to taste

Procedure :

- Prepare the Salad Base:
Wash and dry the mixed greens and berries.
If using larger berries like strawberries, slice them.

- Toast the Nuts (Optional):
For enhanced flavor, lightly toast the chopped nuts in a dry skillet over medium heat for 2-3 minutes until golden and fragrant. Let cool.

- Make the Dressing:
In a small bowl, whisk together olive oil, balsamic vinegar, honey (or maple syrup), lemon juice, salt, and black pepper until well combined.

- Assemble the Salad.

- Dress the Salad.

- Serve.

Nutritions

Calories per Serving: 180 kcal

Protein: 4 g

Fat: 11 g

Carbohydrates: 18 g

Prep Time	:	10 min
Cook Time	:	1-3 min
Servings	:	1 serving

Salad with almonds and oranges

Ingredients :

Mixed greens (e.g., arugula, spinach, or spring mix): 2 cups

Orange: 1/2, peeled and segmented

Almonds (sliced or chopped): 1 tablespoon, toasted

Red onion: 1 tablespoon, thinly sliced

Feta cheese (optional): 1 tablespoon, crumbled

Olive oil: 1 teaspoon

Orange juice (freshly squeezed): 1 teaspoon

Honey or maple syrup: 1/2 teaspoon

White wine vinegar: 1/2 teaspoon

Salt and black pepper: to taste

Procedure :

- Prepare the Salad Base:

Wash and dry the mixed greens and orange.

Peel and segment the orange, removing any membranes.

- Toast the Almonds:

Toast the sliced or chopped almonds in a dry skillet over medium heat for 2-3 minutes until golden and fragrant. Set aside to cool.

- Make the Dressing:

In a small bowl, whisk together olive oil, orange juice, honey (or maple syrup), white wine vinegar, salt, and black pepper until well combined.

- Assemble the Salad.
- Dress the Salad.
- Serve.

Nutritions

Calories per Serving: 160 kcal

Protein: 3 g

Fat: 10 g

Carbohydrates: 15 g

Prep Time :	10 min
Cook Time :	1-3 min
Servings :	1 serving

Salad with sunflower seeds and beetroot

Ingredients :

Cooked beetroot (peeled): 1 medium, diced or julienned

Mixed greens (e.g., arugula, spinach, or spring mix): 2 cups

Sunflower seeds (unsalted): 1 tablespoon, toasted

Feta or goat cheese (optional): 1 tablespoon, crumbled

Olive oil: 1 teaspoon

Balsamic vinegar: 1 teaspoon

Honey or maple syrup: 1/2 teaspoon

Dijon mustard (optional): 1/4 teaspoon

Salt and black pepper: to taste

Procedure :

- Prepare the Salad Base:

Wash and dry the mixed greens.

Dice or julienne the cooked beetroot.

- Toast the Sunflower Seeds:

In a dry skillet, toast the sunflower seeds over medium heat for 2-3 minutes until fragrant and lightly golden. Let them cool.

- Make the Dressing:

In a small bowl, whisk together olive oil, balsamic vinegar, honey (or maple syrup), Dijon mustard (if using), salt, and black pepper until emulsified.

- Assemble the Salad.
- Dress the Salad.
- Serve.

Nutritions

Calories per Serving: 180 kcal

Protein: 4 g

Fat: 10 g

Carbohydrates: 16 g

Prep Time :	10 min
Cook Time :	1-3 min
Servings :	1 serving

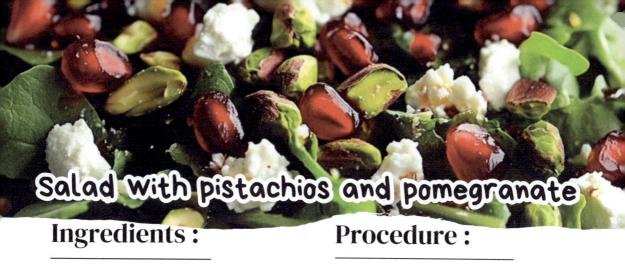

Salad with pistachios and pomegranate

Ingredients :

Mixed greens (e.g., arugula, spinach, or baby kale): 2 cups

Pomegranate seeds: 3 tablespoons

Pistachios (unsalted, shelled): 1 tablespoon, roughly chopped

Feta or goat cheese (optional): 1 tablespoon, crumbled

Olive oil: 1 teaspoon

Pomegranate molasses or balsamic vinegar: 1 teaspoon

Honey or maple syrup: 1/2 teaspoon

Lemon juice: 1/2 teaspoon

Salt and black pepper: to taste

Procedure :

- Prepare the Salad Base:
Wash and dry the mixed greens.
Separate the pomegranate seeds if not already prepared.

- Toast the Pistachios (Optional):
Lightly toast the pistachios in a dry skillet over medium heat for 2-3 minutes until aromatic and slightly golden. Let cool.

- Make the Dressing:
In a small bowl, whisk together olive oil, pomegranate molasses (or balsamic vinegar), honey (or maple syrup), lemon juice, salt, and black pepper until well combined.

- Assemble the Salad.

- Dress the Salad:
Drizzle the dressing evenly over the salad. Toss gently to coat.

- Serve.

Nutritions

Calories per Serving: 180 kcal

Protein: 4 g

Fat: 10 g

Carbohydrates: 18 g

Prep Time	:	10 min
Cook Time	:	1-3 min
Servings	:	1 serving

Peanut and Chicken Salad

Ingredients :

Cooked chicken breast (shredded or cubed): 3 oz (85 g)

Mixed greens (e.g., spinach, romaine, or arugula): 2 cups

Cucumber: 1/4 cup, sliced

Carrot: 1/4 cup, julienned or shredded

Roasted peanuts (unsalted): 1 tablespoon, roughly chopped

Cilantro (optional): 1 tablespoon, chopped

Peanut butter (smooth or natural): 1 teaspoon

Soy sauce (low sodium): 1 teaspoon

Rice vinegar: 1 teaspoon

Honey or maple syrup: 1/2 teaspoon

Lime juice: 1/2 teaspoon

Sesame oil: 1/2 teaspoon

Nutritions

Calories per Serving: 260 kcal

Protein: 28 g

Fat: 11 g

Carbohydrates: 14 g

Procedure :

• Prepare the Vegetables and Chicken: Wash and dry the mixed greens and vegetables.

Slice the cucumber, julienne the carrot, and thinly slice the red bell pepper.

Shred or cube the cooked chicken breast.

• Make the Dressing:

In a small bowl, whisk together peanut butter, soy sauce, rice vinegar, honey, lime juice, sesame oil, and water until smooth and creamy. Adjust the consistency by adding more water if needed.

• Assemble the Salad.

• Dress the Salad:

Drizzle the peanut dressing evenly over the salad. Toss gently to combine.

• Serve:

Serve immediately for a protein-packed, flavorful meal.

Prep Time	:	10 min
Cook Time	:	10 min
Servings	:	1 serving

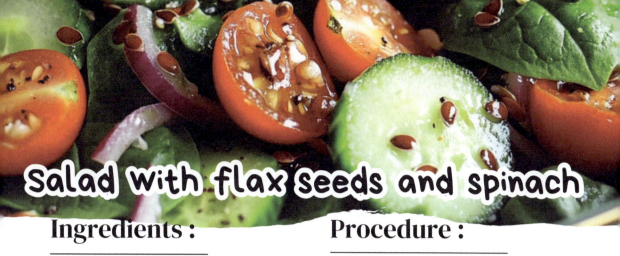

Salad with flax seeds and spinach

Ingredients :

Fresh spinach leaves: 2 cups

Cherry tomatoes: 1/4 cup, halved

Cucumber: 1/4 cup, diced

Red onion: 1 tablespoon, thinly sliced

Flax seeds: 1 tablespoon, toasted

Feta cheese (optional): 1 tablespoon, crumbled

Olive oil: 1 teaspoon

Lemon juice: 1 teaspoon

Honey or maple syrup: 1/2 teaspoon

Dijon mustard (optional): 1/4 teaspoon

Salt and black pepper: to taste

Procedure :

- Prepare the Vegetables:

Wash and dry the spinach leaves.

Halve the cherry tomatoes and dice the cucumber.

Thinly slice the red onion.

- Toast the Flax Seeds:

Toast the flax seeds in a dry skillet over medium heat for 1-2 minutes, stirring frequently, until they are lightly aromatic. Let them cool.

- Make the Dressing:

In a small bowl, whisk together olive oil, lemon juice, honey (or maple syrup), Dijon mustard (if using), salt, and black pepper until emulsified.

- Assemble the Salad.
- Dress the Salad.
- Serve.

Nutritions

Calories per Serving: 250 kcal

Protein: 5 g

Fat: 9 g

Carbohydrates: 12 g

Prep Time :	10 min
Cook Time :	1-2 min
Servings :	1 serving

Salad with pine nuts and broccoli

Ingredients :

Broccoli florets (fresh or lightly steamed): 1 cup

Mixed greens (e.g., spinach, arugula, or spring mix): 1 cup

Cherry tomatoes: 1/4 cup, halved

Red onion: 1 tablespoon, thinly sliced

Pine nuts: 1 tablespoon, toasted

Parmesan cheese (optional): 1 tablespoon, shaved or grated

Olive oil: 1 teaspoon

Lemon juice: 1 teaspoon

Dijon mustard: 1/4 teaspoon

Honey or maple syrup: 1/2 teaspoon

Salt and black pepper: to taste

Procedure :

- Prepare the Vegetables:

Wash and dry the broccoli, mixed greens, and cherry tomatoes.

Steam the broccoli lightly (optional) for 2-3 minutes for a tender texture or use raw for crunch.

- Toast the Pine Nuts:

In a dry skillet, toast the pine nuts over medium heat for 1-2 minutes until golden and fragrant. Let them cool.

- Make the Dressing:

In a small bowl, whisk together olive oil, lemon juice, Dijon mustard, honey (or maple syrup), salt, and black pepper until smooth and emulsified.

- Assemble the Salad.
- Dress the Salad.
- Serve.

Nutritions

Calories per Serving: 190 kcal

Protein: 6 g

Fat: 12 g

Carbohydrates: 13 g

Prep Time : 10 min

Cook Time : 2-3 min

Servings : 1 serving

Salad with pumpkin seeds and pear

Ingredients :

Mixed greens (e.g., arugula, spinach, or spring mix): 2 cups

Pear (ripe but firm): 1 small, thinly sliced

Pumpkin seeds (raw or toasted): 1 tablespoon

Goat cheese or blue cheese (optional): 1 tablespoon, crumbled

Dried cranberries (optional): 1 tablespoon

Olive oil: 1 teaspoon

Balsamic vinegar or apple cider vinegar: 1 teaspoon

Honey or maple syrup: 1/2 teaspoon

Lemon juice: 1/2 teaspoon

Salt and black pepper: to taste

Procedure :

- Prepare the Ingredients:

Wash and dry the mixed greens.

Thinly slice the pear.

If desired, toast the pumpkin seeds in a dry skillet over medium heat for 1-2 minutes until aromatic.

- Make the Dressing:

In a small bowl, whisk together olive oil, balsamic vinegar, honey (or maple syrup), lemon juice, salt, and black pepper until well combined.

- Assemble the Salad.

- Dress the Salad:

Drizzle the dressing over the salad evenly. Toss gently to coat.

- Serve:

Serve immediately for a refreshing and nutritious dish.

Nutritions

Calories per Serving: 180 kcal

Protein: 4 g

Fat: 9 g

Carbohydrates: 21 g

Prep Time :	10 min
Cook Time :	1-2 min
Servings :	1 serving

Chapter 9

Exotic Ingredient Salads

A Burst of Adventure

Exotic ingredient salads feature unique and vibrant ingredients from around the world. With bold flavors and surprising combinations, these salads incorporate ingredients like quinoa, mango, pomegranate, avocado, or dragon fruit, creating a fusion of exciting and refreshing tastes. Often paired with tangy dressings, fresh herbs, and spices, exotic ingredient salads are perfect for exploring new culinary horizons. Whether you're seeking a light, tropical dish or a hearty, flavorful meal, these salads offer a world of possibilities in every bite.

Papaya and Shrimp Salad

Ingredients :

Papaya (ripe but firm): 1/2 small, peeled, and cubed

Cooked shrimp (peeled and deveined): 4 oz (about 6 large shrimp)

Mixed greens (e.g., arugula, spinach, or lettuce): 2 cups

Cucumber: 1/4 cup, sliced

Red onion: 1 tablespoon, thinly sliced

Fresh cilantro (optional): 1 tablespoon, chopped

Olive oil: 1 teaspoon

Lime juice: 1 tablespoon

Honey or agave syrup: 1/2 teaspoon

Fish sauce (optional): 1/2 teaspoon

Salt and black pepper: to taste

Procedure :

- Prepare the Ingredients:

Peel, seed, and cube the papaya into bite-sized pieces.

Slice the cucumber and thinly slice the red onion.

If the shrimp is not pre-cooked, cook them by sautéing in a pan with a small amount of olive oil for 2-3 minutes on each side until they are pink and opaque.

If using fresh cilantro, chop it finely.

- Make the Dressing:

In a small bowl, whisk together olive oil, lime juice, honey (or agave syrup), fish sauce (if using), salt, and black pepper until the dressing is smooth and emulsified.

- Assemble the Salad.
- Dress the Salad.
- Serve.

Nutritions

Calories per Serving: 220 kcal

Protein: 24 g

Fat: 10 g

Carbohydrates: 14 g

Prep Time	:	10 min
Cook Time	:	3-5 min
Servings	:	1 serving

Coconut and Pineapple Salad

Ingredients :

Fresh pineapple: 1/2 cup, cubed

Shredded coconut (unsweetened): 1 tablespoon

Mixed greens (e.g., spinach, arugula, or lettuce): 1 cup

Cucumber: 1/4 cup, sliced

Mint leaves (optional): 1 tablespoon, chopped

Coconut milk (unsweetened): 1 tablespoon

Lime juice: 1 teaspoon

Honey or agave syrup: 1/2 teaspoon

Salt: a pinch

Black pepper: a pinch

Procedure :

- Prepare the Ingredients:

Peel and cube the fresh pineapple into bite-sized pieces.

Slice the cucumber into thin rounds.

If using, chop the fresh mint leaves.

- Toast the Coconut:

Toast the shredded coconut in a dry pan over medium heat for 1-2 minutes, stirring frequently, until golden brown. This step is optional but enhances the flavor.

- Make the Dressing:

In a small bowl, whisk together coconut milk, lime juice, honey (or agave syrup), salt, and black pepper until smooth and well combined.

- Assemble the Salad.
- Dress the Salad.
- Serve.

Nutritions

Calories per Serving: 160 kcal

Protein: 2 g

Fat: 9 g

Carbohydrates: 20 g

Prep Time	:	10 min
Cook Time	:	1-2 min
Servings	:	1 serving

Persimmon and Feta Salad

Ingredients :

Persimmon (ripe, peeled, and sliced): 1 small

Mixed greens (e.g., spinach, arugula, or lettuce): 1 1/2 cups

Feta cheese (crumbled): 2 tablespoons

Walnuts (optional): 1 tablespoon, chopped

Red onion: 2-3 thin slices

Pomegranate seeds (optional): 1 tablespoon

Olive oil: 1 teaspoon

Balsamic vinegar: 1 teaspoon

Honey or maple syrup: 1/2 teaspoon

Lemon juice: 1/2 teaspoon

Salt and black pepper: to taste

Procedure :

- Prepare the Ingredients:

Peel and slice the persimmon into thin wedges or cubes.

Wash and dry the mixed greens.

Slice the red onion into thin rings.

Chop the walnuts (if using) into smaller pieces.

- Make the Dressing:

In a small bowl, whisk together olive oil, balsamic vinegar, honey (or maple syrup), lemon juice, salt, and black pepper until smooth and well combined.

- Assemble the Salad.

- Dress the Salad:

Drizzle the dressing evenly over the salad and toss gently to combine.

- Serve:

Serve immediately as a light, refreshing, and festive salad.

Nutritions

Calories per Serving: 220 kcal

Protein: 6 g

Fat: 16 g

Carbohydrates: 18 g

Prep Time	:	**10 min**
Cook Time	:	**10 min**
Servings	:	**1 serving**

Salad with lotus and seafood

Ingredients :

Lotus root (fresh or pre-cooked, thinly sliced): 1/2 cup

Cooked seafood (shrimp, crab, or scallops): 4 oz

Mixed greens (e.g., arugula, spinach, or lettuce): 1 1/2 cups

Carrot: 1/4 cup, julienned or shredded

Radishes (optional): 2-3, thinly sliced

Coriander or cilantro (optional): 1 tablespoon, chopped

Olive oil: 1 teaspoon

Lemon juice: 1 tablespoon

Sesame oil: 1/2 teaspoon

Rice vinegar: 1 teaspoon

Soy sauce (or tamari for gluten-free): 1 teaspoon

Honey or agave syrup: 1/2 teaspoon

Nutritions

Calories per Serving: 250 kcal

Protein: 25 g

Fat: 10 g

Carbohydrates: 18 g

Procedure :

- Prepare the Ingredients:

If using fresh lotus root, peel it and slice it thinly. If using pre-cooked lotus root, ensure it's properly drained.

Slice the julienne or shred the carrot, and thinly slice the radishes (if using).

If your seafood isn't already cooked, cook it by sautéing in a pan for 2-3 minutes, until opaque (shrimp) or just heated through.

Chop the fresh cilantro (if using).

- Make the Dressing:

In a small bowl, whisk together olive oil, lemon juice, sesame oil, rice vinegar, soy sauce, honey (or agave syrup), salt, and black pepper until the dressing is smooth and emulsified.

- Assemble the Salad.
- Dress the Salad.
- Serve.

Prep Time	:	10 min
Cook Time	:	3-5 min
Servings	:	1 serving

Lychee and Chicken Salad

Ingredients :

Cooked chicken breast (shredded or diced): 4 oz

Lychee (fresh or canned, peeled and pitted): 1/2 cup (about 6-8 lychees)

Mixed greens (e.g., arugula, spinach, or lettuce): 1 1/2 cups

Cucumber: 1/4 cup, thinly sliced

Red onion: 2-3 thin slices

Carrot: 1/4 cup, julienned or shredded

Cilantro or mint (optional): 1 tablespoon, chopped

Olive oil: 1 teaspoon

Lime juice: 1 tablespoon

Fish sauce: 1 teaspoon

Honey or agave syrup: 1/2 teaspoon

Sesame oil: 1/2 teaspoon

Salt and black pepper: to taste

Nutritions

Calories per Serving: 280 kcal

Protein: 30 g

Fat: 12 g

Carbohydrates: 16 g

Procedure :

- Prepare the Ingredients:

If using cooked chicken breast, shred or dice it into bite-sized pieces.

Peel and pit the lychees, and chop them into small pieces if using fresh. If using canned, drain well.

Slice the cucumber and thinly slice the red onion. Shred or julienne the carrot.

If using, chop fresh cilantro or mint for garnish.

- Make the Dressing:

In a small bowl, whisk together olive oil, lime juice, fish sauce, honey (or agave syrup), sesame oil, salt, and black pepper until well combined.

- Assemble the Salad.
- Dress the Salad.
- Serve.

Prep Time	:	10 min
Cook Time	:	5 min
Servings	:	1 serving

Mango and Chili Salad

Ingredients :

Ripe mango (peeled and diced): 1 small

Cucumber (thinly sliced): 1/4 cup

Red bell pepper (thinly sliced): 1/4 cup

Red chili pepper (sliced): 1 small (adjust based on heat preference)

Fresh cilantro (chopped): 1 tablespoon

Lime juice: 1 tablespoon

Olive oil: 1 teaspoon

Honey (optional): 1/2 teaspoon

Salt: to taste

Black pepper: to taste

Procedure :

- Prepare the Ingredients:

Peel and dice the mango into small cubes.

Thinly slice the cucumber and red bell pepper.

Slice the red chili pepper thinly, removing seeds for less heat if desired.

Chop the cilantro for garnish.

- Make the Dressing:

In a small bowl, whisk together lime juice, olive oil, honey (if using), salt, and black pepper until well combined.

- Assemble the Salad.

- Dress the Salad:

Drizzle the prepared dressing over the salad and toss gently to combine.

- Serve:

Serve immediately as a refreshing and spicy salad perfect for a light lunch or as a side dish.

Nutritions

Calories per Serving: 180 kcal

Protein: 2 g

Fat: 8 g

Carbohydrates: 26 g

Prep Time :	10 min
Cook Time :	10 min
Servings :	1 serving

Rambutan and Shrimp Salad

Ingredients :

Rambutan (peeled and sliced): 1/2 cup
(about 3-4 fruits)

Cooked shrimp (peeled and deveined): 4
oz

Mixed greens (e.g., lettuce, arugula,
spinach): 1 1/2 cups

Cucumber (thinly sliced): 1/4 cup

Red onion (thinly sliced): 2-3 slices

Avocado (sliced): 1/4 avocado

Fresh mint (optional): 1 tablespoon,
chopped

Olive oil: 1 teaspoon

Lime juice: 1 tablespoon

Fish sauce: 1 teaspoon

Honey or agave syrup: 1/2 teaspoon

Sesame oil: 1/2 teaspoon

Salt and black pepper: to taste

Nutritions

Calories per Serving: 280 kcal

Protein: 25 g

Fat: 15 g

Carbohydrates: 16 g

Procedure :

- Prepare the Ingredients:

Peel and slice the rambutan into bite-
sized pieces.

If your shrimp is not already cooked, sauté
or boil the shrimp until opaque (about 2-3
minutes per side).

Slice the cucumber, red onion, and
avocado.

If using, chop fresh mint for garnish.

- Make the Dressing:

In a small bowl, whisk together olive oil,
lime juice, fish sauce, honey (or agave
syrup), sesame oil, salt, and black pepper
until well combined.

- Assemble the Salad.

- Dress the Salad.

- Serve:

Serve immediately as a light, tropical salad
perfect for lunch or dinner.

Prep Time	:	10 min
Cook Time :		5-7 min
Servings	:	1 serving

Avocado Chia Salad

Ingredients :

Ripe avocado (diced): 1/2 avocado

Mixed greens (e.g., spinach, arugula, or lettuce): 1 1/2 cups

Cucumber (thinly sliced): 1/4 cup

Cherry tomatoes (halved): 1/4 cup

Red onion (thinly sliced): 2-3 slices

Chia seeds: 1 tablespoon

Lemon juice: 1 tablespoon

Olive oil: 1 teaspoon

Honey (optional): 1/2 teaspoon

Salt and black pepper: to taste

Procedure :

- Prepare the Ingredients:

Slice the avocado in half, remove the pit, and dice the flesh.

Thinly slice the cucumber, red onion, and halved cherry tomatoes.

- Make the Dressing:

In a small bowl, whisk together lemon juice, olive oil, honey (if using), salt, and black pepper until well combined.

- Assemble the Salad:

In a large bowl, add the mixed greens as the base.

Add the diced avocado, cucumber slices, cherry tomatoes, and red onion to the greens.

- Add Chia Seeds:

Sprinkle chia seeds evenly over the salad.

- Dress the Salad.

- Serve.

Nutritions

Calories per Serving: 280 kcal

Protein: 4 g

Fat: 23 g

Carbohydrates: 18 g

Prep Time	:	10 min
Cook Time	:	5 min
Servings	:	1 serving

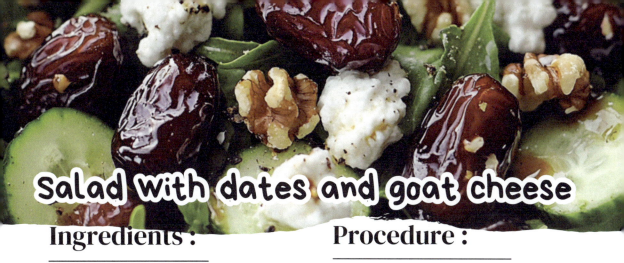

Salad with dates and goat cheese

Ingredients :

Mixed greens (e.g., arugula, spinach, or lettuce): 1 1/2 cups

Medjool dates (pitted and chopped): 3-4 dates

Goat cheese (crumbled): 1 oz (about 2 tablespoons)

Walnuts (chopped, optional): 1 tablespoon

Cucumber (sliced): 1/4 cup

Red onion (thinly sliced, optional): 2-3 slices

Balsamic vinegar: 1 teaspoon

Olive oil: 1 tablespoon

Honey (optional): 1 teaspoon

Salt and black pepper: to taste

Procedure :

- Prepare the Ingredients:

Pit and chop the dates into bite-sized pieces.

Crumble the goat cheese into small pieces.

Slice the cucumber and red onion (if using).

If using, chop the walnuts into smaller pieces.

- Make the Dressing:

In a small bowl, whisk together balsamic vinegar, olive oil, honey (if using), salt, and black pepper until well combined.

- Assemble the Salad.

- Dress the Salad:

Drizzle the prepared dressing evenly over the salad and toss gently to combine.

- Serve:

Serve immediately for a sweet, savory, and crunchy salad.

Nutritions

Calories per Serving: 310 kcal

Protein: 6 g

Fat: 23 g

Carbohydrates: 25 g

Prep Time	:	10 min
Cook Time	:	10 min
Servings	:	1 serving

Chapter 10

Fermented Salads

Tangy, Probiotic-Rich Twist

Fermented salads offer an incorporating experience of the health benefits of fermented vegetables like sauerkraut, kimchi, or pickled cucumbers. These salads are delicious and support gut health, with the natural fermentation process enhancing flavor and digestibility. Often paired with fresh greens, crunchy vegetables, and a zesty dressing, fermented salads bring a unique depth of flavor that's both tangy and satisfying. Perfect as a side dish or a light meal, they are a vibrant and healthful addition to any menu.

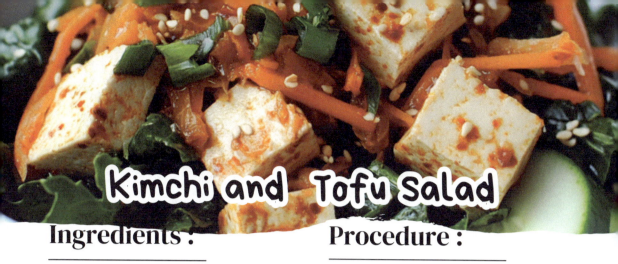

Kimchi and Tofu Salad

Ingredients :

Kimchi (chopped): 1/2 cup

Firm tofu (cubed): 1/2 cup (about 3 oz)

Mixed greens (e.g., spinach, kale, or lettuce): 1 cup

Carrot (julienned or grated): 1/4 cup

Cucumber (sliced): 1/4 cup

Sesame seeds: 1 teaspoon

Green onion (sliced, optional): 1 tablespoon

Soy sauce: 1 teaspoon

Sesame oil: 1 teaspoon

Rice vinegar: 1 teaspoon

Honey or agave syrup (optional): 1/2 teaspoon

Red chili flakes (optional): a pinch

Procedure :

• Prepare the Tofu:

Pat the tofu dry with a paper towel to remove excess moisture.

Optionally, lightly pan-fry the tofu cubes in a non-stick skillet over medium heat for 3-4 minutes until golden (no oil required). Let cool slightly.

• Prepare the Ingredients:

Chop the kimchi into smaller pieces for easier mixing.

Julienne or grate the carrot and slice the cucumber.

• Make the Dressing:

In a small bowl, whisk together soy sauce, sesame oil, rice vinegar, honey (if using), and red chili flakes for a tangy and mildly spicy dressing.

• Assemble the Salad.

• Dress the salad an serve.

Nutritions

Calories per Serving: 180 kcal

Protein: 10 g

Fat: 10 g

Carbohydrates: 12 g

Prep Time :	10 min
Cook Time :	5 min
Servings :	1 serving

salad with sauerkraut and carrots

Ingredients :

Sauerkraut (drained): 1/2 cup

Carrot (grated): 1/2 medium carrot

Green apple (grated, optional): 1/4 apple

Fresh parsley (chopped): 1 tablespoon

Olive oil: 1 teaspoon

Lemon juice: 1 teaspoon

Salt and black pepper: to taste

Procedure :

- Prepare the Ingredients:

Grate the carrot and apple (if using).

Drain the sauerkraut to remove excess

liquid.

- Mix the Salad:

In a large bowl, combine the sauerkraut,

grated carrot, and grated apple.

Add the chopped parsley for a fresh,

herbaceous flavor.

- Make the Dressing:

In a small bowl, whisk together olive oil,

lemon juice, salt, and black pepper.

- Combine:

Drizzle the dressing over the sauerkraut

mixture and toss well to combine.

- Serve:

Serve immediately as a light and tangy

salad, perfect as a side dish or on its own.

Nutritions

Calories per Serving: 90 kcal

Protein: 1.5 g

Fat: 5 g

Carbohydrates: 9 g

Prep Time	:	10 min
Cook Time	:	10 min
Servings	:	1 serving

Salad with fermented cucumbers & potatoes

Ingredients :

Potatoes (boiled and cubed): 1 medium
potato (about 5 oz)

Fermented cucumbers (sliced): 1/2 cup

Red onion (thinly sliced): 2 tablespoons

Fresh dill (chopped): 1 tablespoon

Olive oil: 1 teaspoon

Dijon mustard: 1 teaspoon

Lemon juice or pickle brine: 1 teaspoon

Salt and black pepper: to taste

Procedure :

- Cook the Potatoes:

Boil the potato in salted water until tender
(about 15-20 minutes). Let it cool, then
peel and cube.

- Prepare the Ingredients:

Slice the fermented cucumbers and red
onion. Chop the dill.

- Make the Dressing:

In a small bowl, whisk together olive oil,
Dijon mustard, lemon juice (or pickle
brine), salt, and black pepper.

- Assemble the Salad:

In a mixing bowl, combine the cubed
potato, sliced fermented cucumbers, red
onion, and chopped dill.

- Dress the Salad:

Pour the dressing over the salad and
gently toss until everything is well coated.

- Serve.

Nutritions

Calories per Serving: 180 kcal

Protein: 3 g

Fat: 5 g

Carbohydrates: 30 g

Prep Time	:	10 min
Cook Time	:	20 min
Servings	:	1 serving

Salad with miso and avocado

Ingredients :

Avocado (diced): 1/2 medium avocado

Mixed greens (e.g., spinach, arugula, lettuce): 1 cup

Cucumber (sliced): 1/4 cup

Carrot (shredded): 1/4 cup

Green onion (chopped): 1 tablespoon

White miso paste: 1 teaspoon

Rice vinegar: 1 teaspoon

Soy sauce: 1 teaspoon

Sesame oil: 1 teaspoon

Honey or maple syrup: 1/2 teaspoon

Water: 1 teaspoon (to adjust consistency)

Procedure :

- Prepare the Dressing:

In a small bowl, whisk together the miso paste, rice vinegar, soy sauce, sesame oil, and honey.

Add water to adjust the dressing to your desired consistency.

- Prepare the Ingredients:

Dice the avocado and slice the cucumber. Shred the carrot and chop the green onion.

- Assemble the Salad:

Place the mixed greens on a plate or bowl as the base.

Add the diced avocado, cucumber, carrot, and green onion on top.

- Dress the Salad:

Drizzle the miso dressing evenly over the salad.

- Serve.

Nutritions

Calories per Serving: 180 kcal

Protein: 3 g

Fat: 13 g

Carbohydrates: 12 g

Prep Time : 10 min

Cook Time : 10 min

Servings : 1 serving

Fermented Garlic and Spinach Salad

Ingredients :

Baby spinach (washed): 2 cups

Fermented garlic (minced or thinly sliced): 2 cloves

Cherry tomatoes (halved): 1/4 cup

Red onion (thinly sliced): 2 tablespoons

Crumbled feta cheese (optional): 1 tablespoon

Olive oil: 1 teaspoon

Apple cider vinegar: 1 teaspoon

Honey or maple syrup: 1/2 teaspoon

Salt and black pepper: to taste

Procedure :

- Prepare the Dressing:

In a small bowl, whisk together olive oil, apple cider vinegar, honey (or maple syrup), salt, and black pepper until well combined.

- Prepare the Ingredients:

Wash and pat dry the baby spinach.

Mince or thinly slice the fermented garlic.

Halve the cherry tomatoes and thinly slice the red onion.

- Assemble the Salad:

Place the baby spinach in a serving bowl.

Top with the fermented garlic, cherry tomatoes, red onion, and crumbled feta cheese (if using).

- Dress the Salad:

Drizzle the dressing evenly over the salad.

Gently toss to combine all the ingredients.

- Serve.

Nutritions

Calories per Serving: 110 kcal

Protein: 3 g

Fat: 7 g

Carbohydrates: 8 g

Prep Time	:	10 min
Cook Time	:	10 min
Servings	:	1 serving

Salad with pickled radish and chicken

Ingredients :

Cooked chicken breast (shredded): 3 oz (about 1/2 cup)

Pickled radish (sliced): 1/4 cup

Mixed greens (e.g., spinach, arugula, or lettuce): 1 cup

Cucumber (sliced): 1/4 cup

Carrot (shredded): 2 tablespoons

Sesame seeds (optional): 1 teaspoon

Olive oil: 1 teaspoon

Rice vinegar: 1 teaspoon

Soy sauce: 1 teaspoon

Honey or maple syrup: 1/2 teaspoon

Salt and pepper: to taste

Procedure :

- Prepare the Dressing:

In a small bowl, whisk together olive oil, rice vinegar, soy sauce, honey (or maple syrup), salt, and pepper until well combined.

- Prepare the Ingredients:

Shred the cooked chicken breast.

Slice the pickled radish and cucumber, and shred the carrot.

- Assemble the Salad:

Place the mixed greens on a plate or in a bowl as the base.

Arrange the shredded chicken, pickled radish, cucumber, and carrot on top of the greens.

- Dress the Salad:

Drizzle the dressing over the salad.

Sprinkle with sesame seeds, if desired, and gently toss to combine.

- Serve.

Nutritions

Calories per Serving: 200 kcal

Protein: 25 g

Fat: 6 g

Carbohydrates: 10 g

Prep Time	:	10 min
Cook Time	:	10 min
Servings	:	1 serving

Fermented Ginger and Seafood Salad

Ingredients :

Cooked shrimp or crab meat: 3 oz (about 1/2 cup)

Fermented ginger (thinly sliced): 1 tablespoon

Mixed greens (e.g., spinach, arugula, or lettuce): 1 cup

Cucumber (julienned): 1/4 cup

Carrot (shredded): 2 tablespoons

Avocado (sliced): 1/4 medium avocado

Sesame seeds (optional): 1 teaspoon

Soy sauce: 1 teaspoon

Rice vinegar: 1 teaspoon

Sesame oil: 1 teaspoon

Honey or maple syrup: 1/2 teaspoon

Chili flakes (optional): a pinch

Procedure :

- Prepare the Dressing:

In a small bowl, whisk together soy sauce, rice vinegar, sesame oil, honey, and chili flakes (if using). Set aside.

- Prepare the Ingredients:

Thinly slice the fermented ginger.

Julienne the cucumber, shred the carrot, and slice the avocado.

- Assemble the Salad:

Place the mixed greens on a plate or in a bowl as the base.

Add the cooked shrimp or crab meat, cucumber, carrot, and avocado.

Top with the fermented ginger slices.

- Dress the Salad:

Drizzle the dressing evenly over the salad.

Sprinkle with sesame seeds for garnish.

- Serve.

Nutritions

Calories per Serving: 210 kcal

Protein: 18 g

Fat: 10 g

Carbohydrates: 12 g

Prep Time	:	10 min
Cook Time	:	10 min
Servings	:	1 serving

Salad with pickled peppers and beans

Ingredients :

Cooked kidney beans or black beans (drained and rinsed): 1/2 cup

Pickled peppers (sliced): 2 tablespoons

Mixed greens (e.g., spinach, arugula, or lettuce): 1 cup

Cherry tomatoes (halved): 1/4 cup

Red onion (thinly sliced): 2 tablespoons

Olive oil: 1 teaspoon

Lemon juice: 1 teaspoon

Ground cumin (optional): a pinch

Salt and pepper: to taste

Procedure :

- Prepare the Ingredients:

Rinse and drain the cooked beans if needed. Slice the pickled peppers, halve the cherry tomatoes, and thinly slice the red onion.

- Assemble the Salad:

Place the mixed greens in a bowl or on a plate as the base.

Add the beans, pickled peppers, cherry tomatoes, and red onion on top.

- Make the Dressing:

In a small bowl, whisk together olive oil, lemon juice, cumin (if using), salt, and pepper.

- Dress the Salad:

Drizzle the dressing over the salad and toss gently to combine.

- Serve:

Serve immediately as a refreshing and tangy salad with a mix of bold flavors.

Nutritions

Calories per Serving: 180 kcal

Protein: 7 g

Fat: 6 g

Carbohydrates: 25 g

Prep Time :	**10 min**
Cook Time :	**10 min**
Servings :	**1 serving**

Fermented Horseradish & Beetroot Salad

Ingredients :

Cooked beetroot (cubed or grated): 1 medium beet (~1/2 cup)

Fermented horseradish (grated or paste): 1 tablespoon

Mixed greens (e.g., arugula or spinach): 1 cup

Walnuts (chopped): 1 tablespoon

Goat cheese (optional, crumbled): 1 tablespoon

Olive oil: 1 teaspoon

Apple cider vinegar: 1 teaspoon

Salt and pepper: to taste

Procedure :

- Prepare the Ingredients:

If using fresh beetroot, cook and cool it beforehand. Cube or grate it as desired. Chop the walnuts for added crunch.

- Assemble the Salad:

Place the mixed greens on a plate or in a bowl as the base.

Arrange the beetroot over the greens.

Add the fermented horseradish, scattering it evenly over the salad.

- Add Toppings:

Sprinkle the chopped walnuts and crumbled goat cheese (if using) over the salad.

- Make the Dressing:

In a small bowl, whisk together olive oil, apple cider vinegar, salt, and pepper.

- Dress the Salad.

- Serve.

Nutritions

Calories per Serving: 180 kcal

Protein: 5 g

Fat: 8 g

Carbohydrates: 17 g

Prep Time	:	10 min
Cook Time	:	10 min
Servings	:	1 serving

Salad with pickled apple and walnuts

Ingredients :

Pickled apple (sliced): 1/2 medium apple (~1/4 cup)

Mixed greens (e.g., arugula, spinach, or lettuce): 1 cup

Walnuts (toasted and chopped): 1 tablespoon

Cranberries or raisins (optional): 1 tablespoon

Feta cheese (optional, crumbled): 1 tablespoon

Olive oil: 1 teaspoon

Apple cider vinegar: 1 teaspoon

Honey or maple syrup: 1/2 teaspoon

Salt and pepper: to taste

Procedure :

• Prepare the Ingredients:

Slice the pickled apple thinly for easy layering.

Toast the walnuts in a dry pan over medium heat for 2–3 minutes to enhance their flavor.

• Assemble the Salad:

Place the mixed greens on a plate or in a bowl as the base.

Arrange the pickled apple slices over the greens.

Sprinkle the toasted walnuts, cranberries or raisins, and crumbled feta cheese (if using) on top.

• Make the Dressing:

In a small bowl, whisk together olive oil, apple cider vinegar, honey, salt, and pepper.

• Dress the Salad.

• Serve.

Nutritions

Calories per Serving: 180 kcal

Protein: 4 g

Fat: 11 g

Carbohydrates: 18 g

Prep Time	:	10 min
Cook Time	:	10 min
Servings	:	1 serving

Chapter 11

Healthy Salad Sauces

Tangy, Creamy, and Savory

Healthy salad sauces are the perfect way to elevate any salad with flavor while keeping it light and nutritious. These dressings are rich in healthy fats, vitamins, and antioxidants and and made with wholesome ingredients like olive oil, avocado, yogurt, tahini, or citrus. They add depth and complexity without the heaviness of traditional store-bought options. From a simple lemon vinaigrette to a flavorful tahini dressing, healthy salad sauces provide the perfect balance of taste and nutrition, making every salad a delicious and satisfying meal.

Lemon Olive Sauce

Ingredients :

Olive oil: 1 tablespoon

Lemon juice: 1 tablespoon (freshly squeezed)

Lemon zest: 1/2 teaspoon

Garlic (minced): 1 clove

Green olives (pitted and chopped): 4–5 olives

Dried oregano: 1/4 teaspoon

Salt and pepper: to taste

Fresh parsley (optional, chopped): 1 teaspoon

Procedure :

- Prepare the Ingredients:

Mince the garlic and chop the green olives. Zest and juice the lemon.

- Make the Sauce:

In a small bowl, combine the olive oil, lemon juice, and lemon zest.

Add the minced garlic, chopped olives, and oregano to the bowl.

Stir everything together until well mixed.

Season with salt and pepper to taste.

- Optional Garnish:

Stir in some fresh parsley for extra flavor and color.

- Serve:

Drizzle the sauce over grilled vegetables, chicken, fish, or pasta. Serve immediately.

Nutritions

Calories per Serving: 130 kcal

Protein: 0 g

Fat: 14 g

Carbohydrates: 3 g

Prep Time	:	5 min
Cook Time	:	5 min
Servings	:	1 serving

Balsamic Vinaigrette

Ingredients :

Balsamic vinegar: 1 tablespoon

Olive oil: 2 tablespoons

Dijon mustard: 1 teaspoon

Honey (or maple syrup): 1/2 teaspoon

Garlic (minced): 1 clove

Salt: a pinch

Freshly ground black pepper: to taste

Procedure :

- Make the Vinaigrette:

In a small bowl, whisk together the balsamic vinegar, Dijon mustard, honey, and minced garlic until smooth.

Slowly drizzle in the olive oil while continuing to whisk, until the dressing emulsifies and thickens slightly.

- Season the Vinaigrette:

Add salt and pepper to taste, adjusting to your preference.

- Serve:

Drizzle over your favorite salad or roasted vegetables. Stir well before serving if the dressing has separated.

Nutritions

Calories per Serving: 150 kcal

Protein: 0 g

Fat: 14 g

Carbohydrates: 4 g

Prep Time	:	5 min
Cook Time	:	5 min
Servings	:	1 serving

Mustard - honey sauce

Ingredients :

Dijon mustard: 1 tablespoon

Honey: 1 tablespoon

Apple cider vinegar: 1 teaspoon

Olive oil: 1 teaspoon

Garlic powder: 1/4 teaspoon

Salt: a pinch

Freshly ground black pepper: to taste

Procedure :

- Combine the Ingredients:

In a small bowl, whisk together the Dijon mustard, honey, and apple cider vinegar until smooth.

- Add the Oil and Seasoning:

Slowly drizzle in the olive oil while continuing to whisk, ensuring the mixture emulsifies.

Add the garlic powder, salt, and pepper, and whisk to combine.

- Serve:

Use the sauce as a dip for vegetables, drizzle over grilled chicken or salads, or spread on sandwiches.

Nutritions

Calories per Serving: 100 kcal

Protein: 0 g

Fat: 7 g

Carbohydrates: 9 g

Prep Time : 5 min

Cook Time : 5 min

Servings : 1 serving

120

Tahini and Lemon Sauce

Ingredients :

Tahini (sesame paste): 2 tablespoons

Lemon juice: 1 tablespoon (freshly squeezed)

Garlic (minced): 1 small clove

Olive oil: 1 teaspoon

Water: 2-3 tablespoons (to thin the sauce)

Salt: a pinch

Freshly ground black pepper: to taste

Procedure :

- Combine the Tahini and Lemon Juice:
In a small bowl, whisk together the tahini and lemon juice. The mixture may thicken initially, which is normal.

- Add Garlic and Olive Oil:
Add the minced garlic and olive oil to the mixture, and whisk until smooth.

- Thin the Sauce:
Gradually add water, one tablespoon at a time, until the sauce reaches your desired consistency. If you want a thicker sauce, use less water; for a thinner dressing, add more.

- Season the Sauce:
Add a pinch of salt and freshly ground black pepper to taste. Whisk again to combine.

- Serve:
Drizzle the sauce over roasted vegetables, salads, grain bowls, or grilled meats.

Nutritions

Calories per Serving: 180 kcal

Protein: 5 g

Fat: 15 g

Carbohydrates: 6 g

Prep Time :	**5 min**
Cook Time :	**5 min**
Servings :	**1 serving**

Horseradish and sour cream sauce

Ingredients :

Horseradish (prepared, not fresh): 1 tablespoon

Sour cream: 3 tablespoons

Lemon juice: 1 teaspoon

Dijon mustard: 1/2 teaspoon

Garlic powder: 1/4 teaspoon

Salt: a pinch

Freshly ground black pepper: to taste

Procedure :

- Combine the Ingredients:

In a small bowl, mix together the sour cream and horseradish until smooth.

- Add Seasoning:

Stir in the lemon juice, Dijon mustard, garlic powder, salt, and black pepper. Whisk until fully combined and smooth.

- Adjust the Consistency:

If the sauce is too thick, add a small splash of water or more lemon juice to achieve the desired consistency.

- Serve:

Use the sauce as a dip for roasted meats (like roast beef), grilled vegetables, or as a topping for baked potatoes.

Nutritions

Calories per Serving: 90 kcal

Protein: 1 g

Fat: 8 g

Carbohydrates: 3 g

Prep Time	:	5 min
Cook Time	:	5 min
Servings	:	1 serving

Conclusion

How to Add Variety to Your Salads

Salads can be a delightful mix of textures and flavors, but adding variety can transform them from mundane to exciting. To start, experiment with different greens—swap romaine for arugula, kale, or spinach for a fresh twist. Incorporate seasonal vegetables for color and crunch; think roasted beets, grated carrots, or sliced radishes. Mix fruits like apples, berries, or citrus to balance the savory flavors.

Vary your dressings too—switch between vinaigrettes, creamy sauces, or a simple squeeze of lemon and olive oil for a lighter option. Mixing up these components will keep your salads exciting and full of variety.

Useful Tips for Storing Ingredients

- Herbs: Store fresh herbs like parsley and cilantro in the fridge in a jar of water (like a bouquet). Cover loosely with a plastic bag to keep them fresh longer.
- Vegetables: Root vegetables like potatoes, carrots, and onions should be stored in a cool, dark place in ventilated containers. Store tomatoes at room temperature for the best flavor, but refrigerate them once they're fully ripe.
- Leafy greens: To keep greens like spinach or lettuce crisp, place them in a clean towel inside a container to absorb moisture.
- Grains and nuts: Store these in airtight containers in a cool, dry place. Refrigeration is recommended for nuts, especially in warm weather, to prevent them from going rancid.

By organizing your ingredients properly, you can reduce spoilage and maximize the flavor of your dishes.

Inspiration for Creating Your Own Recipes

- Creating your own recipes can be a rewarding and fun experience. To start, think about what ingredients you love and how you can combine them in new ways. Focus on balancing flavors—sweet, salty, bitter, sour, and umami. For instance, pair a tangy vinaigrette with roasted vegetables or combine creamy avocado with spicy salsas for a fresh twist.

- Get creative with cooking techniques—try grilling, roasting, or even fermenting ingredients you'd usually steam or sauté. Don't forget texture! A dish with a mix of crispy, creamy, and crunchy elements is often the most satisfying.

- If you're ever stuck for inspiration, look to different cuisines. Experiment with spices or flavor combinations from Italian, Indian, or Middle Eastern cooking. And always taste as you go—small adjustments can elevate your creation into a unique dish that's all your own.

Appendix

Useful Tips for Choosing Ingredients

Choosing high-quality ingredients is the first step to making delicious meals. Here are some tips to help you select the best ingredients:

- Fruits and Vegetables: Choose produce in season for the best flavor and value. Look for vibrant colors and firm textures—soft or wrinkled produce may be overripe. If possible, buy fresh, sustainable options from local farmers' markets.
- Meat and Fish: Look for fresh cuts with a good amount of marbling (for beef) or clear, bright eyes and firm flesh (for fish). Always smell seafood before purchasing—anything that smells off is likely spoiled.
- Dairy: Check expiration dates and avoid dairy with any off smells or curdling. When selecting cheese, please ask for a sample to check its flavor profile.
- Grains and Beans: For dry ingredients like grains and beans, choose ones with a clean, unbroken appearance and store them in airtight containers to maintain freshness.

By selecting the freshest and best-quality ingredients, your meals will have that extra touch of flavor that makes all the difference.

Recommendations for Combining Products

Great cooking is all about finding harmonious combinations of flavors, textures, and ingredients. Here are some recommendations for pairing ingredients that elevate your dishes:

- Sweet and Savory: Combine sweet elements like fruits (apples, figs, or citrus) with savory items like cheese, roasted meats, or nuts. Think arugula and pear salad with blue cheese or pork with apple sauce.
- Herbs and Spices: Fresh herbs like basil, thyme, and rosemary add brightness to dishes, while spices like cumin, cinnamon, and paprika deepen flavors. A spice rub on roasted vegetables or grilled meat can elevate your dish, while fresh herbs sprinkled on top add a burst of freshness.
- Crunch and Cream: Combining textures is a great way to enhance a dish. Pair crunchy elements like nuts or croutons with creamy ingredients like avocado, hummus, or yogurt. A classic example is a creamy dressing drizzled over a crunchy salad.
- Acid and Fat: A balance of acid (like lemon juice or vinegar) and fat (like olive oil or butter) can make a dish shine. Try squeezing lemon on roasted vegetables or a splash of vinegar in a creamy dressing to bring everything together.

Experiment with these combinations to discover the perfect pairings for your recipes!

Made in United States
Troutdale, OR
04/16/2025

30667714R00071